A Handful of Straw Blowing in the Wind

By
Thelma Doak

Love Thelma Doak, mich 2007

Dedicated to my late husband, Bob and to our children,
June, Jean, Bob, Donn, and their spouses Frances, Doug,
Shirley and Gene. A special thanks to dear friends Dave
and Anneke Kayfes and Dorris Budzier.

ISBN No
978-0-9791550-3-1
About Time Publishing
First Printing
February 2007

What life is sometimes,
A handful of straw blowing in the wind.

When life comes to an end,
All you have accumulated,
All you have is
A handful of straw blowing in the wind.

— Thelma Doak
Jan. 24, 2007

Foreword

I was teaching my Beachside Writer's Workshop in Yachats and asked participants to tell a little bit about themselves so we could get to know each other.

"I was born in 1903 in Oklahoma," said a woman with a storyteller's voice. "Well, at the time it wasn't Oklahoma. It was Indian Territory."

I imagined the two dozen participants doing the math: My gosh, this woman is 102 years old!

But as the weekend unfolded, what amazed the participants — and me — wasn't how old Thelma Doak was. But how well she wrote. How well she remembered. And how diligently she focused both on the stuff that matters: people, places and the times that connect the two.

By the end of the weekend, only one writer had been given a standing ovation: Thelma Doak. I don't need to tell you she's a writer; the pages that follow will show you.

True, she has seen the Wright brothers in person, heard John Philip Sousa's band play and watched Halley's Comet streak across the sky in 1910. But Thelma's story isn't about her having lived a long time, but lived so well. So passionately. So absolutely intent on surviving — and enabling her family to survive — despite dust-bowl odds that wilted or killed so many.

Her story is about perseverance. Second chances. In the words of Dylan Thomas, refusing to "go gentle into the good night."

At 96 and taking care of a 75-year-old daughter - you never stop being a mother - Thelma realized that she needed some "taking care of" of her own. Elder Help, a Eugene, Oregon organization, sent her a volunteer to help her do errands so she could keep living at her home.

She didn't like its choice. The volunteer was, well, a man. His name was Dave Kayfes, then 57.

He mentioned that he liked composting; turns out, Thelma had composted long before it was cool. She warmed up a bit.

He told her he was a retired Register-Guard sportswriter. She warmed up a bit more. Seems Thelma had written a few things herself. Once had a poem published in the Denver Post and a few tidbits in weekly newspapers. And had puttered away on an overview of her life.

Kayfes read the piece and was impressed. She had written that her life's happiest times had been living in a dust-bowl house in Colorado during the Depression and raising four children with her husband, Bob. "But the Good Lord watched over us and we learned the greatest lessons in our young lives - the meaning of true friends and good neighbors, caring, sharing and helping each other in steadfast love."

At an Elder Help Christmas party in 2000, Thelma unwrapped a present to find her hand written pages typed and collated in a plastic binder. By Dave.

As she was leaving, she told a staff person that Elder Help was like the three swans on a lake in Colorado where she had once visited. As temperatures dropped and the ice formed from the outside in, the swans would paddle in circles so their warmth and movement would slow the expansion of ice, would stave off the inevitable.

She teared up and gave Dave a playful backhand to the shoulder. "He's my swan," she said.

He encouraged her to write an actual book. She hesitated. He prodded. Finally, she started it, knowing that the ice was hardening fast.

It became her quiet crusade: to finish this book about these hard but good years. She wrote of dust storms blowing through the house so fiercely that rooms "became as dark as a cellar when a flashlight fails." Of saving bloated cows by stabbing them with a knife and jamming a tube near their hip bone. Of making burial garments after a neighbor boy died.

After Thelma hand-wrote a chapter, Kayfes would type it into a computer. He encouraged her to go to writing workshops. Reluctant at first, she did so. That's where I had the privilege to meet her. Two years later, on her 104th birthday, I had the privilege of spending time with her again.

I told her she was leaving the world a wonderful legacy — not only with these words she'd written, but the life she'd lived.

Never famous. Never seeking the spotlight. Never full of pride. Just a woman who placed others above herself. Who helped raise a family, and who, late in life, had the courage and drive to write a book about overcoming hardships that would have defeated less courageous folks.

We live in a live-for-the-moment world in which people are increasingly ambivalent about the importance of legacies. "We are fast losing the sense of historical continuity, the sense of belonging to a succession of generations originating in the past and stretching into the future," wrote Christopher Lasch in The Culture of Narcissism.

Thelma Doak reminds us of the importance of remembering that past. For older people, particularly those who faced the same or similar hardships, this book will unlock their own stories. And for younger people, some of whom think that real trouble is, say, not being able to find a TV remote, this book will offer perspective.

And for the woman who wrote it? I believe it represents a small dream-come-true that, with Kayfes' help, she had nurtured for nearly a decade.

Now that the book is finished just days after her 104th birthday — "you should have seen the look on her face when I gave it to her," said Kayfes — I couldn't help but think this:

It's as if all the words that needed to be said have now been said and all the stories that needed to be written had now been written.

And the swans could leave the lake with no regrets.

Bob Welch
Register-Guard columnist

3

Prologue

We left behind us a magnificent view of the Twin Spanish Peaks in the Sangre de Cristo Mountain Range. They nudged the shoulder of the Colorado Rockies and were soon lost in the shimmering heat waves of the summer of 1974.

"This trip to the 'East End' will be a big surprise," my son told me.

I knew he alluded to the southeastern area of Las Animas County, Colorado, where the local people always referred to the area as the "East End." I could not believe it had been 50 years since I had visited that locality.

Time and distance passed quickly in the comfort of Bob's new Oldsmobile and pleasant conversation concerning his home and geology work in Trinidad. There was no traffic, no detours, no speeders, no eager-beaver in-and-out drivers, no stops for a cold Coke or to use wayside restrooms. I don't remember the villages being so far apart; the area seemed so unfamiliar and empty to me now. I suppose being accustomed to years of noise, clamor and the hurry-hurry business of life in towns and cities made this 100-mile trip a rarity of peaceful tranquility.

Once we glimpsed a crumbling skeleton of a rock building. A few miles farther, we observed a lone Mexican herding a straggling flock of sheep. As the shepherd stooped to pet his sheep dog, Bob smiled at me. "If it hadn't been for his big bright-colored sombrero, that fellow would have been hidden by the tall grass in that landswag," he said.

Bob left the highway and parked on a grassy incline. Glancing around me, I saw the cobalt-blue Mesa de Mayo that hugged the state line between Colorado and New Mexico — *That was all*. The sky, with heart-aching clarity and grace, met the earth to form an unblemished horizon for miles and miles. It must have been like this in the beginning, I thought. When God created this land and said, "It is good."

"Where are we?" I asked.

"It's the old Tobe community. See that dead tree? It's the one aunt Mabel started from a marshmallow roasting stick she pushed into the ground. It grew in the front yard of her home and the Tobe Post Office."

"It's gone — everything, everywhere," I cried out. This was not the anticipated surprise but a heart-stopping shock. I closed my eyes. A strange sensation of the earth zig-zagging in slow motion gripped me.

"What happened here?" I demanded in a shakey voice. "Where are all of the homes? The people? The fences? The windmills? The cattle that grazed on the lush prairie grass in the spring and drank from the shallows where buffalo wallowed years ago? They couldn't disappear like magic."

There was no river — not even a big creek to flood and sweep everything away. No tsunami. What a ridiculous thought: The Pacific Ocean is 1,000 miles away. There is no record of a great fire; twisted, tortured metal objects would be visible everywhere.

My son stood near me, his hands clasped before him as though he waited for a benediction.

Before he could answer any of my questions, the silence was shattered by a loud squawk and the flurry of feathers as a pheasant flew from the tall grass. A young deer startled by the commotion, sprang up from a cluster of sun-scorched weeds, gave us a brown, glassy-eyed stare and bounded gracefully from our sight.

"Mother, the East End communities are gone. There's nothing left but the grass." He pointed to a large white sign with Mesa de Mayo forming the backdrop in the distance. I read outloud

COMMANCHE
Federally-owned Grassland

A time, a place, a way of life that is gone forever belongs to history; to the stories told for many years by many people from many places — and from my own experiences.

In the 1890s, the United States government gave free grazing rights for thousands of acres of primitive prairie grassland that waved like a wheat field in a breeze to western cattlemen. The JJ Ranch, owned by the Jones brothers, moved its large herd from the Arkansas River Valley, headquartered at Higbee, Colorado, to eastern Las Animas County, Colorado.

Their "dollar-a-day" and "glad to get it" cowboys built bunk houses, strung barbed-wire fences, treated injured cattle, guarded them from coyotes, mountain lions, timber wolves and gangs of cattle thieves. They heckled the chuck-wagon cooks when beans rattled on their tin plates from being cooked in the hard water; praised him to the sky for "larrupin" crispy-crust fried pies with dried apricot and dried peach fillin'. "M-m-m-uh. So good, made you want to slap your grandpappy," one Texas cowboy declared.

Sweaty, saddle-sore and weary at the end of the day, sometimes, when there was no place for entertainment, they sang by a campfire accompanied by a battered guitar, harmonica and the twang of a Jew's harp — songs of home, lonesome days, lonely nights, lost loves and "somebody's done somebody wrong" cowboy ballads.

Ears perked up when an old-time, bow-legged, trail-scarred cowpoke told of early encounters with Billy The Kid and Blackjack Ketchum, desperados of the early Wild West. "The Kid" killed 21 men to avenge the mistreatment of his mother before he was killed by a New Mexico sheriff.

One of the less familiar stories he told concerned a Sister of Mercy nun, Sister Blondina Segale. When one of The Kid's gang lay near death in an abandoned adobe shack on the outskirts of Trinidad, a coal-mining town and county seat, The Kid forced the sister to nurse the man back to health. In return, he promised she would never be harmed by his gang on her stagecoach journeys to church in Santa Fe, and her driver would never suffer a holdup. When later he recognized her in an approaching stagecoach, he tipped his hat and signaled his gang to "take to the hills." He never reneged on his promise, she wrote in her book, "The End of The Santa Fe Trail."

Blackjack Ketchum, after a long siege of bank and train robberies, cattle stealing and murders, was captured and sentenced to be hanged. From the jail window in Clayton, New Mexico, he watched men building the scaffold for his execution. "I wish they'd hurry," he remarked. "I want to get to hell in time for dinner."

The JJ cattle herd grazed, fattened and produced many calves. All went well until the sheepmen brought their flocks to graze in the same area.

What started as a tit-for-tat nuisance developed into a ferocious range battle between cowboys and sheep herders. Cattlemen filed for homesteads and fenced the water holes, making them inaccessible for sheep. Their cowboys used every means of chicanery to drive the sheep herders out of the area. With six-shooters spitting fire, whoops and "yippies," Stetson hats slapping saddle leather, they spooked the bleating flocks, crowded them in fenced corners and over the canyon's edge, where hundreds perished.

The sheep herders retaliated by cutting fences, contaminating water holes, disfiguring cattle brands. They sicked their snarling, barking sheep dogs on the cattle. In horror and wild confusion, the cattle panicked and stampeded. The cattlemen experienced tremendous loss.

The grassland became over-grazed when other cattle companies began to move their herds into the region. A great range war erupted and continued for years with tremendous loss on all sides. The JJ herd numbered in the thousands of cattle by this time. New calves increased the numbers yearly. Overgrazing became an issue, which added fuel to the problems already out of control.

"It's the cowboys," the Mexican sheep herders declared. "B-e-e-g cows eat much grass — same place."

"It's the dad-gum Mexican herders," the cowboys said. "The sheep nibble — nibble the grass down to the roots. They cook in summer, freeze in winter. Hot wind, no rain for days added to the problem.

Regardless of whom was to blame, the grasslands, expected to last forever, eroded slowly. With the market glutted, the price for cattle fell to a one-hundred-year low. The carnage and mayhem of the long range war, the obvious loss of livestock and lives were sacrificed to appease the greed and hatred of men fighting over the God-given gift of grass.

In 1903 and again in 1910 and 1914, devastating panic gripped the country. Anguished people — homeless, jobless, down to their "last thin dime," with hungry, hollow-eyed, half-clad children, whose tattered shoe soles were patched with cardboard and laced with twine — cried out for help. In an effort to quell the restlessness and fomenting anger, to prevent a disastrous-looming outcome, the government opened the west for homesteading.

A flood of covered wagons poured westward with people to claim 320 acres of land. The government offered this 'haven for the homeless' with few requirements for ownership and no limitations. Real estate companies presented a glowing picture of the country with no mention of the scarcity or water, the bitter cold winters, the man-and-beast-killer blizzards, the anger and frustration of the resentful cattlemen.

When the JJ ranchers, reduced now to a remnant of their earlier holdings, heard the news they were furious. "The dirt farmers have no right here," they said. "It's grazing land. Always was. Always should be."

They did have a right, a legal one, the dirt farmers maintained. "The cattlemen could take it or lump it; the dirt farmers were here to stay."

Undaunted by threats, harassment, arguments, the determined farmers built temporary homes, dugouts, half dugouts, part underground structures with a lumber overhead of three feet, houses of soddy blocks of grassland, adobe bricks, logs and rocks from the canyons. In the punishing winter of 1914, the homesteaders were trapped in an unusual blizzard weather pattern. The heavy snow prevented trips to the nearest town. Food supplies were gone. People were hungry.

While Lillie Brown, a nine-year-old girl, watched for strangers at the farm gate, her father and a neighbor butchered a JJ fat steer. Others did the same to feed their hungry families. The roving JJ cattle had demolished crops. The farmers felt justified and claimed it was just compensation for the damage.

The JJ enterprise dwindled. Cattle, cowboys, bunkhouses, chuck wagons gradually disappeared and the get-rich-quick cattle era ended.

In 1914, war broke out in Europe. The demand for wheat exploded and the price reached an all-time high of four dollars a bushel. Farmers everywhere began to plant wheat. The dirt farmers also took advantage of the rush. Plows ripped from the land the rich native grassland that grew in wild profusion for years. Farmers plowed and planted. Tractors were introduced and 50 acres of wheat became 100, 500 and 1,000-acre fields with vacant land owned by many of the young men who went to war with the government's promise to issue a deed for their service.

When America entered the war, people thought good times would last forever. Lured by the buy-now-pay-later mentality, new homes, new cars, anything desired could be bought "on time." The war ended in 1918 and the big boom ended; banks failed, mortgages were foreclosed, payments came due, unheard-of unemployment followed. A total collapse occurred when the stock market crashed in 1929 and the Great Depression swept the country like a prairie fire. . .

On the return trip to Trinidad, Bob and I talked and talked. As far as viewing the scenery was concerned, we might as well have been travelling in the Sahara Desert, it claimed so little of our attention.

There had been other trips in recent years. Just the two of us, mother and son reconnecting after the nurturing years of his life centered on home, family and career. Our time together now was special, precious.

We recalled names of neighbors and long-time friends: The Dixons, Bryants, Reagans, Beans, Mohons, Whites, Ballards, Greens, Stocktoons. Who could forget grandma Dixon? A shouting Methodist whose fervor made us want to clap our hands and sing "Tis the Old Time Religion."

Still shocked, drained by remorse, by what we had seen this day, I could not begin to imagine the heartache., the smothering sadness of loss. I was reminded of the little boy who was asked where his folks would go. With his big brown eyes locked in innocence, he shook his head and answered: "God only knows."

A New Home

In the early morning of Sept. 1, 1932, we finally arrived at an abandoned house on 320 acres of land near Villegreen, Colorado. This was to be our home during what we hoped would be the end of the lingering Depression.

Bob, my husband, with our four-year-old son, Bobby, stopped the loaded truck near a yard gate swinging precariously by one hinge; a second one dangled from a fence post. I parked the Chevrolet I drove with our two little girls, June and Jean, and our almost two-year-old baby, Donny.

"We're here," the children shouted as they exploded from the car like chickens released from a coop. Before I could say, "Be careful," they headed for an old cellar with a slanted door. With whoops and squeals, they took turns running up and down the door as creaks, groans and rattle of boards filled the air.

If those old weathered boards break, it will be the first of many accidents in this hapless place, I told myself.

After two days of — "How much farther is it to our new home?" "When are we going to get there?" "I'm hot." "Make Bobby put the window up. It blows my hair." "I want a drink." "I need to pee pee." "Donny smells bad." — I was in no hurry to get out of the car. I felt I was stuck to the seat. I didn't want to look at the house either. I looked away to the flat-topped mesa to the south, to the distant west where I could see the faint outline of a long mountain range, white-crested by an early snow. To the east there was nothing but barbed-wire fences and grass, stubby grass browned by a long hot summer.

My husband waited. I had stalled as long as I could.

"No neighbors," I said weakly — part statement, part questioning.

"Sure, there's neighbors. You just can't see them from here," he assured me as he opened the car door.

I forced myself to look at the house, an unpainted L-shaped wooden structure setting on rocks for support and enclosed by a sorry-looking fence. It sagged between posts like a much-overworked hammock. The yard was grassless, treeless, wind-swept and dusty. Looking behind me, I saw a small barn with a sway-back roof, a shed, I presumed built to function as a garage, a tiny chicken house constructed of small logs dabbed with adobe mud to fill gaping cracks. A pole-fenced corral and a windmill that creaked eerily as it pumped reddish water into a concrete tank completed the picture.

A sickening feeling stirred in the pit of my stomach. I didn't know anything about a farm. Any preconceived picture I had in my mind didn't resemble this.

I looked at Bob. Instantly, the look in his hazel eyes told me we were sharing the same thoughts as our minds traveled back to the home we left two days ago. I saw the stucco and brick-trimmed house, the closely-cropped Bermuda grass lawn, the cozy living room with a gas log burning in the fireplace in the winter, the sunny dining room, the kitchen with an ice-box replenished every other day by an ice man who read the card in the window. I could hear the low whistle of Mack, our ice man, at the backyard gate, then the chip-chip-chip and splinter of ice before he put a sliver in the eager outstretched hand of each girl. He looked up, saw me standing near. "Didn't quite fit," he said. You faker, I thought. You said that the last time and the time before.

I pictured the rainbow colors of marigolds, zinnias, petunias. The dainty smell of Four O'clocks that misted the evening air with their fragrance and showcased their beauty. Without the abundance of pure clear water, the profusion of flowers would have withered and died weeks ago.

Now, a glance at the slightly-leaning chimney on the roof brought me back to the house a few footsteps in front of me.

"No one but a rank amateur could build a chimney that crooked," I said.

"Let's go inside and take a look before we unload," Bob said.

The children joined us as we entered the unlocked weathered door. A white porcelain knob came loose and clattered to the floor. Squeak, squeak, squeak echoed through the empty rooms as we walked cautiously over rough and gritty floors. Wall paper drooped from corners. Smudgy windows, like giant eyes, glared at us, threatened us for the abrupt intrusion in their hazy light of dusty emptiness.

"Why are we whispering?" Bob laughed, which broke the weird silence.

"You tell me," I answered with a forced bit of laughter. "Smells musty. Empty houses always give me the creeps," I said, lifting the corner of the fly-specked wallpaper.

"Good grief," I said, my voice sounded like it came from a foghorn. The kids came running. "B-e-ed bugs." I pressed the flap of wallpaper quickly to the wall as a bug attempted to scoot farther underneath the paper.

"Whew. It stinks." I wrinkled my nose, made a wry face and shuddered.

"Daddy, I saw a bed bug, too," Bobby announced excitedly as he came running from the storage room on the back porch.

"What did it look like?" I asked.

He held up his thumb and forefinger about one inch apart. "This big," he said. "Had a hard black shell and a long snout."

My husband looked at me quickly, raised his eyebrows and rolled his bugged-out eyes. I was relieved to see his usual merriment return, which helped to remove some of the tension I was feeling.

"Wow, son! That's too big for a bed bug. Not quite big enough for a snapping turtle."

"Better watch it," I cautioned when Bobby was out of sight. "our renters may have made many good friends when they lived here. Some day your son may tell his playmates: 'My daddy said we found bed bugs as big as turtles when our renters left.' You might come up with a lump on your head, saying: 'Whoda' thunk it?'"

We had a good laugh, a much needed tonic. We finished our tour of the three-room house.

"This place has to be fumigated, scalded, scraped and scrubbed clean before we bring one thing from the truck."

"I'll turn the chickens out of the crates, feed the rabbits, then we'll get started," he said.

The rabbit and chickens idea had been promoted by some of Bob's friends, who kept needling him with glowing pictures of our honey-pond and fritter-tree adventure.

I felt more inclined to listen to a sage old farmer we knew in Texas. He shifted a wad of tobacco in his mouth and spit on the ground. With gnarled thumbs in his overall bibs, he began his comments:

"The way things 'er goin', you'd better get a liken' for

flapjacks and corn-cob jelly. That's what us old farmers, poor as the devil, are eatin'."

Fortunately, our renters had left an old-fashioned half-way respectable wood range in the kitchen. It looked sturdy. The fire box was intact, the oven still hinged, the big hot water reservoir rusty but in one piece and would hold water. The warming oven was filthy but undamaged otherwise. The range was badly in need of a good cleaning to remove the grease and grime. We were glad to have it.

It was amazing how much we accomplished with hot water from the cleaned reservoir and cleaning supplies from a country store one and a half miles from our northwest quarter-acre.

By late afternoon, after much elbow grease and hard work, the bare house had windows that sparkled in the sun. Floors were scrubbed down to yellow pine freshness with lye, soap and hot water. Walls were brushed clean, the wall paper pasted and patched to an unbelievable make-do-for-awhile condition. A pleasant smell of refreshing antiseptic cleaners permeated every inch of the house.

From the truck we brought the roll of black and white checked linoleum and covered the kitchen floor. The delft-blue enameled table and chairs were next. They gave a cheerful splash of color to the north end of the big kitchen. The living room came to life quickly with the first piece of furniture — a convertible couch which would have to serve as a third bed at night, a large oak desk, an occasional table, a red and black cut-velvet chair, a Cogswell chair and matching stool and the Victrola fit nicely in the room without making it overly crowded. A large plate-glass mirror hung on one wall reflected the whirling windmill near the corral.

After the rug was layed in the bedroom, the apple-green furniture and an extra bed were placed on the opposite wall, a chest set between the beds before a window, a sewing machine doubled for an extra table. Although I regretted petulantly that so many things had to be left behind because there was no space in the truck, there was no room here for another thing.

By suppertime, a cheerful fire roared in the old range, sporting a fresh coat of polish. The reservoir steamed and hissed and helped to chase away the chill of the autumn evening. A gasoline lamp, a relic from Bob's homesteading days hung from the tongue and groove wood ceiling and cast a soft light over us as we bowed our heads when the time came for one of our children's turn to say grace. Thoughts of the simplicity, the peace of that moment — familiar things in new surroundings — made my heart beat wildly. How many people, homeless, hungry, cold and almost ready to give up, would be happy to be in our place? Right then, in spite of my many misgivings, I promised as a loving wife and mother I was ready to accept the challenge to make a happy home here if it killed me.

After ten days we were going in circles — two steps forward, one step back. The girls began a new experience in the one-room school house. The two and one-half miles was too far for them to walk, which meant two car trips each day. An old friend from homesteading days loaned us Daisy, a black and white Holstein cow, which made it possible for us to have milk and butter. I even forgave the Leghorn pullet in one of the coops on the truck on our trip to the farm. She cackled and cackled, causing a big ruckus as we were passing a funeral procession in Amarillo, Texas. She had laid her first egg. Evidently, she wanted the hearty congratulations of her peers. I scooted down in my seat behind the steering wheel and wished for a place to hide. I knew we were a sight for unbelieving eyes — that old truck loaded to the top with furniture, rolled rugs and linoleum, two chicken coops, one on top of the crates with canned fruit and a sack of unripe yellow tomatoes above it; the other lashed to the back of the truck, side by side with a chicken wire pen holding a couple of nose-twitching Chinchilla rabbits.

I began to wonder if we were ever going to get settled when

my parents came from Oklahoma in a surprise visit to give us some help and moral support. They had the experience and know-how we lacked.

When the Indian territory was opened for settlement in the early 1890s, my parents homesteaded a 160-acre claim. They were young with limited means, limited farm experience and three small children - one a baby in mother's arms. It was a constant struggle to make a home and to eke out a decent living. The wilderness was an area of sandhills, rattlesnakes and five-inch scorpions, coyotes, deer, prairie dogs, scrub oak and chinery thickets. Sand and cockle burrs matted the horses' tail and brought smarts to the children's bare feet. Chiggers and red ants created never-ending itching and scratching for the annoyed children.

What my folks lacked in experience they balanced with courageous fortitude, self-reliance and hard work. Without the benefit of a physician and the help of a neighborhood midwife, I was born a hefty 12-pounder in 1903. When my father bargained for the service of the horse and buggy doctor, the old man was very emphatic I learned years later:

"No doctor, unless he is as crazy as a coot, would drive 14 miles to deliver a baby in a blizzard. It's January. We'll wait and see...."

My father was a fixer. He could perform miracles with bits and pieces and a few seemingly worthless parts. After listening one evening to his homestead stories and Bob recalling his own experience, on Monday morning they began the work of restoring our badly neglected place. First they made a windlass from scraps of old lumber, a log and heavy rope to draw the rusty pipes from the well enabling us to have clean clear water. Bob had been hauling barrels of water from a neighbor's spring for our household use, which consumed much of his time.

Next, the shameful roof of the barn was propped up and loose boards re-nailed. Stables were built in lieu of the horses we would own some day. Harness racks, storage bins for the corn and pinto bean seed left from the renter's lease went up fast from salvaged lumber. Pinon poles that lay rotting on the ground were replaced with new ones for the corral. The slow leak in the stock tank was patched with new concrete.

The rabbits settled into their new hutch that stood on legs to keep them off of the ground on chilly nights. The chicken house was cleaned and new nests filled with sweet-smelling hay. As an incentive for the pullets to get going with their egg-laying business, dad tucked a shiny China egg in the nests. We culled the flock of chickens after a lesson by the county agriculture agent on the technique for determining which pullets would be the good egg-layers. The roosters and rejected-pullets were canned with a borrowed pressure cooker.

The men made a truck trip to the Arkansas River valley below the caprock at La Junta. They returned tired but jubilant over their marvelous purchase at the truck farms. Five bushels of red apples for 50 cents each, five cents extra for washing; 100 pounds of crisp cabbage for one-half cents a pound, a penny a pound for potatoes and onions. The deal was sweetened by two gallons of two dollar and fifty cent honey and a bucket of home-made cane sorghum molasses.

"What in the world will we ever do with all of this cabbage?" I asked.

"You'll see," my father answered. "We're going to make kraut."

"Probably make enough to furnish the restaurant at Kim for a year," mother said.

And make kraut, we did. The cabbage was shredded and packed in a five-gallon stoneware crock with layers sugared and salted. Dad made a mallet from a piece of oak he found after a long search. When the bruised cabbage, pounded by the mallet, made sufficient liquid to rise to the top of the crock the job was about finished and all of the cabbage gone, except some to be used prudently for coleslaw and a cooked vegetable. The crock was capped by a plate weight my father made with a washed rock, then covered with a white cloth tied tightly with a twine string. Nothing was left but a lengthy wait for fermentation and the finished product.

Over a bed of fresh hay, the apples were poured from the sacks and scattered at the back of the cellar. With the shelves of the colorful jams, jellies, preserves and pickles I had made before we left our former home, the cellar looked somewhat like a country fair exhibit.

"The corn in the crib has a thick husk," my father announced. "That means a bad winter. It's time mom and I should go home."

"I sure don't want to get caught in one of those notorious blizzards," mother commented.

We had worked from the rooster's morning crow to bedtime. There had been little time left for thinking about the coming winter storms.

"We could never have done all of the work by ourselves," Bob said as he thanked them for their expertise, labor, good advice and company.

We watched their car disappear down the lane.

"It will be lonely for you now. The girls in school and I'm gone so much," Bob said.

"With two rambunctious boys, you gotta' be kidding. Lonesome? Yes, at times, but not for long. Most anything can happen without one minute notice.

"And, some day, when you find yellow corn growing on a red cob, I'll make corn cob jelly. I promise."

Farm Life

The children took to farm life like piglets to a mud puddle.

Having visited their grandfather's farm, they were not typical "city kids." They were unlike my three-year-old nephew, who saw a rag picker and horse-drawn cart for the first time. His mother explained about horses: "They were used long before cars," she told him. His inquisitive mind demanded more detail. "Where do they put the gas in?" he asked.

My children knew very little about farms and animals, but they did know horses needed no gasoline, milk didn't come from bottles and eggs did not come from trees just because an egg fell out of a tree where a pair of old hens roosted on grandpa's farm.

They explored the barn. They climbed the corral fence, walked the concrete rim of the empty stock tank. Chickens squawked. Pigs squealed and ran like ants from a disturbed colony hill to avoid the onslaught.

"Mother, come quick! We found a nest in some cornstalks behind a haystack. There's a whole gob of eggs," my oldest called.

A white Leghorn pullet with motherly instincts had stolen her nest away from the straw-lined ones in the hen house. In lieu of a brood of peep-peeping babies, she chose to hatch them in the seclusion of a secret place. It was an unexpected treat to find so many eggs in one nest.

In their eagerness to get an early count on daily egg production, they slipped into the hen house during the afternoon. With a slow, careful approach they reached under warm fluffy feathers to feel the eggs in the nest. Ouch! They were rewarded with an unexpected sharp peck that left them with smarting fingers and a degree of humiliation. So much for interfering with her domestic duties.

"Am too big a'nough," two-year-old Donny insisted in spite of his sister's protest that he was more hindrance than help. He began to cry when June refused to let him help put eggs in the bucket.

"All right, here's an egg."

Plunk. Crackle. Crunch.

"Look what Donny did, Mother! He put an egg in the bucket like it was a rock."

I took the bucket, emptied the contents into a mixing bowl and picked out the shells. Presto-chango. Pre-scrambled eggs ready for breakfast. Donny soon forgot his need to be a helper and began to look for more exciting ventures.

Daddy work. Mother work. Children work made acceptable by naming their part-"chores."

The girls brought baskets of spicy-scented white and red cedar chips to build fires and replenish dying ones. Bobby, arms piled to his chin with range-length cedar and pinon, tossed his burden into the woodbox by the range.

Determined not to miss one thing, they followed Daddy to the corral for milking time. Each wanted a turn at sitting on the teetery stool, anticipating a big stream of milk to add to the billowing foam in the pail. Time after time, the result was the same. Puff and grunt. Pull and squeeze. The cow waited patiently while dissipating-foam in the bucket went flat and not one spoonful of milk made it to the bucket when the experience was over.

"It's easy. Like this," Bob told the children as the lesson

started the same way each evening with hands-on instruction.

Lucky for us. Had we lived in town, the entire neighborhood would have been alerted with Jean's announcement one evening.

"Mother, I got my first squirt from a cow," she shouted thinking her accomplishment was worthy of the top prize as far as she was concerned.

Churning presented a new challenge.

"Use one hand only for each of you." I showed them how to grasp the dasher of the big iron stoneware churn. Before I had time to say, "scat," to our nosey black and white cat, they grabbed the dasher and began an agitated wobble that threatened to overturn the churn and spill thick clots of cream on the linoleum.

"No, no! It takes team work." I placed my hand with theirs on the dasher. "Everybody ready — up, down, up, down. See how easy it is when we all work together?"

For a few minutes it made fun. With their short span of interest and with churning excitement less than chasing pigs, their experience fizzled.

"I haf' to go to the bathroom."

"I need to feed the rabbits."

"I help." Donny trailed after his brother.

Jean wanted to look at her reading book.

So, June and I were left with the churning.

"It takes too long," June complained after a few ups and downs.

"Sing to the churn." I took the dasher and started in a sing-song rhythm.

"Peter's at the garden gate. Waiting for a butter cake. Come butter come."

I could tell she was not impressed with my song and had doubts of its effectiveness to produce golden mounds of butter. Peter could wait. She was too young to give a hoot about his amorous intentions.

"Go play with the others. It's almost done. I'll finish." I showed her the yellow flecks on the dasher.

Curiosity had been satisfied. There was no enthusiasm left for a boring procedure. I was left to gather the golden globules, wash and mold the butter and pour the tart buttermilk into a pitcher.

Happy to have churning time to myself thereafter, I could listen to Caruso or John McCormick sing love songs on the Victrola — undisturbed.

I'll never forget that first rain after we came to the farm.

The entire area from the front gate and windmill to the corral and barn, to the kitchen door resembled one sea of squishy mud. Mud. Mud Mud everywhere. Not one thick patch of grass the size of a bedsheet could boast of being mowed like a lawn; not one foot of sidewalk anywhere to remind us of our home in Texas.

The children hated it. They were accustomed to paved streets, sidewalks and Bermuda lawns. They found this adobe mud turned as slick as that mouse that fell in our lard bucket. They slipped and had to be rescued. The animals splattered mud. I was forever having to hold a wriggly child who stood on one foot like a horse to be shod, while I scrapped the sticky stuff from shoes and bare feet.

I often thought I might be able to duplicate adobe with one part chewing gum, one part boiled okra and one part terra firma — found elsewhere not on this farm — to stabilize the mixture. That would be asking for a miracle.

With the children's dislike for it and obvious disgust, they were prompted to label every sticky, gooey, gummy, messy and abhorrent substance — M U D.

My pedal sewing machine needed oil, but in my haste to finish the dress I had been trying to finish for two weeks, I decided to tolerate the raspy whir a few more minutes.

What was that? I listened; stopped pedaling and caught my

breath. Someone crying. Sounded like Donny, who was playing with the others near the barn. That old pile of lumber waiting to be cleared away. Maybe he had stepped on a nail.

I ran to the door.

His sister, as petite for her age as he was large for his two years, was leading him gently by the hand toward the house. He struggled to walk on one foot and the heel of the other. There appeared to be no sign of blood or panic, just loud crying.

A mother learns to distinguish the nature of baby and childhood cries by the time number four arrives. She recognizes a hungry cry, an angry cry, a sleepy cry, a cry of fear or terror, the feverish whimper of a sick child. She experiences the agonizing pain herself when there is an injury or illness and there is no cry at all.

He saw me standing by the gate and began to blubber, pleading for what sounded to me like sympathy and a much-needed nap.

"I 'tep in old chickie mud," he wailed and looked down at the repulsive goop squished between his chubby toes.

Poor little guy. His sleepy eyes were smudged with dark circles where he had rubbed them with grubby fists. Snot and tears mingled and trickled down his dirty face.

I gathered him up in my arms and took him to the kitchen, a haven for hurts, complication and treatment with soap and water. The soothing touch of the soft cloth and warm water relaxed him and weakened his sobs to a sleepy sniffle.

When the last trace of the offending mess disappeared in the murky greenish water of the wash pan, we headed for the rocking chair.

I knew a wonder-working panacea for a little buckaroo whose dignity had been terribly diminished by a misstep. What blissful comfort for the babe — and the mother — I thought as I held his warm body in my arms and began to rock and sing.

"Sweet and low. Sweet and low. Winds of the Western Sea... Blow him again to me. While my little one while my pretty one sleeps."

I moistened my finger at my lips as I had seen my mother

and countless others do and coaxed spit curls in his unruly hair.

I love to rock babies. I hope there will be rocking chairs in heaven and babies, like my granddaughter's pleading: "Wock, grandmommy, wock."

"He'll have to learn to be careful," Bob told me when I related the chickie mud story to him. "The farm's no place for sissies."

"Hmmmm, I'll have to remember that — good advice," I assured him.

After the rain ceased, the girls and Donny avoided the corral. The spring deluge had turned the pastures into a lush green paradise for the animals. An over indulgence of the succulent green grass caused the cattle to develop a bovine malady called Scours. The feedlot became a slimy mire-zone.

Bobby, his father's shadow, sat on the pinon-pole fence to watch the calves hunch, slobber and slurp at their mother's udder. Separating the calves from the mothers after feeding time was no easy matter and most often resulted in a chase and capture routine. The slimy corral complicated the task even more than usual.

I heard my husband shouting to the rollicky calves. I saw Bobby coming to the house doing his best to suppress a broad grin on his freckled face.

"Mother, you should see Daddy. He was chasing a calf. He fell flat down in the nasty corral."

I looked up from my button-hole making. Bob stepped gingerly on his way to the house. As he held the bib of his overalls away from his body with his thumbs, his lips were curled in disgust. When he saw me, he looked down at the green mess dripping toward his knees. "Don't you dare come in here," I called to him and made no attempt to refrain from laughter.

"Go to the garage. I'll bring clean clothes to you."

Be careful. Sometimes it's much easier to give advice than to take it, I cautioned the children. Watch your steps.

Ho hum! It's been a busy day.

Ollie

The school day ended at 4 o'clock. After the ride home, the girls bounced into the kitchen where I was busy making early preparations for our supper. In their eagerness to be first to recount the day's excitement, they practically fell over one another.

"This funny kid named Ollie had a fight today. The teacher spanked him with a board."

"Yea-h-h, she just punished the other kid — made him stay after school."

"The big kids won't let Ollie play with them. They throw rocks at him."

"Nobody chooses him when we play anti-over and Farmer in the Dell. He's 'dopted, the big girls said."

"The big boys call him 'dummy and snot nose' 'cause he's got a cold."

"Sh-h-h," I put my fingers to my lips. "One at a time, please."

"He oughta be in the fourth grade. The teacher says he misses school too much. The big girls say Ollie's different."

I interrupted. I was shocked by the children's candor. It sounded to me like they might be influenced by some big girls' talk, which closely resembled grown-up gossip.

"How is Ollie different?" I asked.

"His boots are dirty and laced all crookedy. His shirt tail

always hangs out, His pants are split. His hands are black and cracked, and his hair is ratty."

This description came from our chatterbox second grader, who walked around on tip toes as soon as she took her first steps because she didn't want to get her feet dusty. She acted almost as fastidious as she was petite.

"Once he burned some library books 'cause he didn't want to go to school, the big kids said."

"Yea-h-h. The big girls said 'cause he's 'dopted sometimes he has to stay all-l-l by hisself."

"And sometimes he has to stay home from school to work."

"Sounds to me like Ollie needs some good friends," I said. This required more attention than I could give at the time. I shooed them off to the bedroom to change their school clothes to play ones.

With water scarce and having to carry it bucket by bucket from the weak well, pour it into a barrel and "break it" for laundry day presented a big task. A daily head-to-toe change of clothing for four children became impossible. Sometimes I dreamed of being in our former home, turning the water faucets on full blast in the kitchen sink to watch the water gurgle down the drain.

Breaking water became another new task for me. Our weak well, over-used and abused inspite of cleaning, had huge amount of minerals in the water, especially iron. Without breaking, it looked rusty with a slight metallic taste. When used with soap, it turned into the consistency of buttermilk.

"Will it kill chickens?" my visiting sister-in-law asked as she made a wry face and spit the big gulp of water on the ground. She liked to brag about their "wonderful soft water" on their ranch in New Mexico.

In our semi-arid country, water was a precious commodity. If it was drinkable, reasonably safe health-wise, and you were as thirsty as a dog exhausted after chasing a jack rabbit, who quibbled over taste?

We added common household lye, the same kind we used to make soap, to the barrel of water at night. In the morning, a pink sponge-like foam, almost an inch thick, lay on top of the water. When it was skimmed away, the result was water, undrinkable because of the caustic lye, but clear and safe as from a natural spring.

No more white clothes that looked like they had been dabbled in a muddy creek. Colors were bright and smelled of spring freshness. After much frustration and loss of temper a few times, a good neighbor — bless her — taught me to "break the water." A clothesline of dazzling whites and bright colors fanning in the breeze can bring an unspeakable joy to a mother's heart. It's uncanny that small details in life can bring so many unexpected pleasures. I often thought of this and counted my blessings.

Bob had come into the kitchen in time to hear part of the Ollie story.

"You girls be nice to Ollie," he said. "I don't want to hear that you have ever been unkind to him. Hear?"

When I was sure the children were out of sight and couldn't hear us, we began to talk.

"You know children," I said. "Big ears. Big eyes. Big bumps of curiosity, a tendency to imitate. It scares me — this daily mix of big kids and little kids, big boys and big girls at this tender age.

"Well, they aren't going to learn to live in the big world of adults any younger are they? We're going to have to set good examples of love and trust for them.

"I never did get to tell you what happened when mother and dad visited us, did I?"

He shook his head negatively.

"One day after school, the children were giving me their daily accounts of activities. June went to the bedroom to change her clothes, but our chatterbox remained with mother and me. Jean began to describe the little houses on the far side of the schoolhouse

— one for girls, one for boys. 'The big girls call them back houses and privies. There's a bench with two big holes and a little one.'

"I interrupted her: 'I think toilet is a much nicer word, don't you?' She shook her head in agreement.

"She continued, 'I held up one finger like the teacher said if you needed to go to the bath — er, toilet. When I got out there, a big girl was there just sitting. She said she had to shit, and there wasn't any paper. I nev-v-er heard it called that!'

"Mother was standing at the cabinet peeling potatoes. She started to reach for another potato, but popped her hand over her mouth instead. She made her big brown eyes full of surprise and rolled them towards me.

"'Go change your clothes, please,' I told my daughter. 'We'll talk about school later. Right now I need to help grandmother with supper."

Bob listened, waiting for another new problem in our farm life.

I knew if I made an issue of what Jean had said, she would be embarrassed and it might destroy her confidence later when we needed to talk.

"'Uh, oh,' mother said. 'Looks like she's going to learn something besides readin', writin' and 'rithmetic. She's such a timid little one, you know she wouldn't have said that word before me had she known something was wrong with it.'"

I finished the story and sighed deeply. "Sometimes I wonder if we did the right thing by moving to the farm — this mix of big kids and little kids. Children need to learn from their parents, not from the flip mouths of big girls.

"We weren't exactly bombarded with solutions to our problems, were we?"

"It's time to do the milking," Bob said. He grabbed the milk bucket and gave a near slam to the door as he left for the barn. I noticed our nerves were becoming edgy at times. I was inclined to be the one easily upset when problems appeared tough. Bob was the calm one and his show of annoyance at this time alarmed me.

Did he think I blamed him for the Depression and the loss of our new home in Texas?

Who is to blame when history reverses itself and repeats its troubles? Why did my paternal grandparents lose their ranch and thriving cattle business in the Panic of 1893? Who was to blame when my parents lost everything but our home in the "hard times" of the early 1900s — and the beginning of World War I? What was to blame for the Depression of 1910-12, for the crash of the stock market in 1929? There's enough blame to go around in each case of failure, hopelessness and dwindling of the middle class in our country.

As usual, I began to reminisce, a habit I have tried to break. The bare one-room school house, built by volunteers in the early days, made a sharp contrast to the one in the college town where we had lived in the Texas panhandle. The girls had gone to kindergarten and first grade at summer school, which was taught by enthusiastic teachers from the college training department. Lush potted plants and baskets of flowers gave a colorful glow to their class rooms. A huge sand table with various kinds of interesting things — buckets, shovels, scoops and toys. There were miniature tables and chairs, cuckoo clocks, colored sticks, building blocks, bells; things to hear, feel, touch and smell to keep children occupied.

The main incentive involved teaching them to share, to help, to learn to play together happily. It proved to be a fun place.

There were no big kids and little kids. No big girls and little girls. All of them were from middle-class families in a small midwestern college town. The people living there were neither rich nor poor - just good neighbors quick to respond when help was needed. No brown-black-white racial problems or long-time feuds or grudges. They were so much alike their unique differences made no enemies to cause fights and to destroy relationships.

They took their churches, school and politics seriously. Democrats and Republicans might let their arguments become a little testy at election time, but when it ended, they joked, slapped backs and forgot them, never leaving traces of anger or bitterness.

A $2 poll tax kept some from voting. Others deliberately refused, citing the injustice of having to pay to vote. Republicans were denied voting privileges because there was no ballot printed for them in our overwhelmingly Democratic state.

City dads were forceful without being bullies, town folks could disagree without meanness, fist fights and hair pulling. Women at times might appear to be clannish, but they could work together without being nasty and hurtful. There was no need for a curfew in this little town. Parents set their own limits and guidelines for their families and cooperated to see they were followed. Children flocked to all the movies. If they couldn't read the picture titles, they still enjoyed them. The entire town celebrated when the first talkie came to our own movie theater...

Time to stop recalling our life that "used to be" and concentrate on the here and now.

A few weeks later, a bitter wind that pinched noses and numbed fingers blew out of the north.

"The sky's as blue as your fountain-pen ink," Bob said to me as he piled a big fresh-cut load of wood into the box by the range.

"Gonna snow," he told the children. "Since it's Saturday, we'll play games tonight."

"Goody, goody, goody," they yelled in unison and clapped their hands gleefully.

Dinner, our noon meal, was almost ready. Bob opened the door to put his boots in the storage place on the back porch. We heard the clatter of horse's hoofs on the frozen ground.

"Hello there," he called to a young boy who dismounted

from a saddled pony and looped the reins over the gate post.

"It's Ollie," I heard one of the girls whisper.

"Lookin' for a lost cow," the boy said haltingly. His half-buttoned jacket hung off one shoulder, wisps of scraggly dull hair escaped from the navy blue cap pulled down over his ears. I knew it was Ollie before I heard the whisper. Impressed by the handsome pony and the expensive-looking saddle, I thought: Somebody loves this 'dopted boy.

"You can have dinner with us," I said when he came inside.

"My folks mightin' like it," he said.

"Oh, I'm sure they wouldn't mind at all - it's such a cold day. You have all afternoon to find the cow."

He looked at the table, skewed his mouth to one side. "Well, I guess it'll be okay." He removed his cap and plaid jacket, insisted he lay them on the floor by the wood box.

"Girls, please set a place at the table. Ollie is going to be our guest."

Ollie jerked his head quickly, looked at me and his quizzical look faded to a broad grin.

Usually, a squabble occurred over which girl would set the plates and which would arrange the knives, forks and spoons. Without any argument, they went about the task in angelic cooperation and grown-up precision. Ollie watched them with apparent interest.

Bob made his usual preparation for mealtime as he washed his face and hands and combed his hair at the washstand near the back door.

"Boys, come. Let's get ready for supper." He ushered them toward the washstand, where he had placed a gray granite pan filled with fresh warm water from the range reservoir. He made generous use of soap and water for Donny. As usual, Bobby had imitated his father's procedures and stood waiting for the regular hair combing.

Ollie watched with rapt attention. Bobby's hair, which seldom looked uncombed, was finished quickly. Donny's tousled and unruly hair could have had a bird's nest built in it had he stood still long enough. It took more time and brought loud protests.

"Ouch! That pulled! I got hair in my eyes."

When the combing was done, Bob refilled the wash pan. "Want to wash up?" he asked nine-year-old Ollie.

Ollie stepped up to the washstand, cupped his hands as Bob had done, splashed water on his face, and gave his hands a quick rub together. He took the proffered towel, hurriedly mopped his face and gave his hands another quick twist in the towel.

"Better get them real dry or they'll chap," Bob cautioned Ollie.

I shuddered as he took Ollie's hands — dark, cracked, resembling stale cornbread, over-baked and crusty — in his own and patted them gently until they were completely dry.

"Maybe I can help you with that part," Bob offered as he watched the boy wince as he pulled the comb held in his fist across the back of his head.

Without a word, he handed Bob the comb. Bob worked carefully on the tangles as Ollie watched in the mirror over the washstand. Bob dampened the comb and parted his hair on the side exactly as he had done for his sons.

"Different," the girls had said. There was nothing a little attention and TLC couldn't fix. I looked at the three boys' shining faces, hair combed as sleek as a fresh-groomed calf as they sat at our table.

"Jean, it's your turn to say grace," Bob said. Ollie glanced at the bowed heads, hesitated a second, then tucked his chin to his chest and closed his eyes.

"Do you have any brothers?" I asked, attempting to engage Ollie in conversation.

"Huh-uh," he answered.

"Any sisters?" He shook his head.

Soon he became relaxed and began to talk. "Onc't my folks wuz gone at night I couldn't get my boot off. I tried and tried. The string had a big knot in it. Makes my mama mad if I break the strings. So, I just wrapped my muddy boot in a towel and went to bed. Didn't get the bed one bit dirty, neither. Mama didn't ever know it. I hid the towel," he added, evidently pleased with his own solution to a muddy problem. He looked at us with a mischievous grin.

"You have a beautiful pony," Bob said.

"Yep, my uncle gave it to me for my birthday. He's good to me. Daddy gave me the saddle."

He finished eating and pushed his chair away from the table.

"Gotta find the cow 'fore my folks git back."

Bob held his jacket for him, making sure it was zipped up to his chin, and handed him his cap and mittens.

"Goodbye, Ollie, come to see us again," we called to him and watched as he climbed upon his snorting, stomping, impatient pony.

Ollie was never our guest again. Later, he accompanied his mother to the county seat, 100 miles from their home, to pay taxes and do some shopping. On their way home in the dark cold night, the car blew a tire.

While Ollie was standing near the car holding a flashlight so his mother could see to change the tire, a fast-travelling vehicle loomed out of the darkness, zig-zagged and side-swiped their car.

"I don't know how long I lay there. When I called to Ollie, he didn't answer," his mother said after she returned from the hospital.

Earlier, state police, noting erratic behavior, stopped the car of a late-night traveler. They found bits of clothing and fresh blood on the front bumper. They decided to investigate.

They found Ollie's injured mother underneath the car and Ollie in a nearby ditch with the flashlight, still glowing, clutched in his small fist.

Barter

"There's a man living near the mesa. He's leaving the country. Bad crops. Bad health. Wants to trade livestock and farm machinery for a truck. I think I'll go to see him."

"Good luck," I called to him and waved goodbye as he drove away.

It would require a tremendous amount of luck to get rid of that old rattle trap. I would have equipped him with a four-leaf clover or rabbit's foot had either been available. I should have told him: "trade for a load of wood, food, anything we can use." It reminded me of things I was anxious to forget — the sooner, the better. We could not afford to keep that truck, even if we needed it, which we didn't. Where was the money for gasoline to run it?

Besides, who would want that old relic? If that man expected to get to some special place in a hurry, he was asking for trouble. Maybe he's a mechanic, I thought.

With its yellowish green paint peeling from the battered body, the spoke wheels, skinny tires and motor tucked under a dented hood, it was a perfect picture of unloving care and neglect.

Bob always insisted each of the traders should get a good bargain, so he offered our new stucco-and-brick-trimmed home in Texas for two thousand dollars and the truck. I was appalled at the audacity of his price offering.

"Times have changed," my husband said and the deal was

closed without further consideration.

I had mixed feelings when that truck appeared in our driveway back home. My optimistic husband insisted the motor had been replaced "not long ago," whatever that meant, and was in "good shape;" whatever that meant I had no idea.

"With a little tune-up, it will purr like a pussy cat."

We had purchased used cars before, which needed "just a little tune-up." We had them tuned up and tuned up to the tune of the price of a new car before the tuning was done. As the repairman patted his money pouch on the way to the bank in his new Cadillac, we limped down the street in our tuned-up Chevrolet.

One thing Bob had in his favor — he had an honest face and business-like demeanor. His friend said: "I'd trust that guy with the keys to the U.S. Treasury."

"Well, my dear, I'm thinking, that's a good endorsement when you're peddling a lemon. However, that man might be skittish about dealing with a complete stranger. But he might be satisfied to get a less-than-lovely truck in order to get away before winter. It did get us to the farm. It was still running.

I glanced at the clock. "It's 5 o'clock. I wonder if daddy's had truck trouble." June was playing jacks on the kitchen floor.

I hardly finished the sentence when Bobby yelled over his shoulder as he ran toward the big gate.

"Mother, daddy's here. Looks like a train coming down the road."

If I live to be 110, I'll never forget that scene — the Great Depression on Wheels.

Bob was sitting in a wagon pulled by two big mules with three horses tethered to the wagon. A long line of farm implements, each attached to one in front of it — as Bobby said, like a train. I gave my mind a vigorous jolt and saw box cars and a caboose trailing a long banner of dust — not smoke.

In a race to meet daddy, I got there first.

"Honey, that man gave me everything he had for that truck. Well, almost everything, but a saddle and his wife." Happiness was written in big letters all over his face. "I drove a hard bargain for that saddle. It was a beauty. Great leather. Fancy tooling. Silver trappings. I really wanted it."

"And the wife?" I rolled my eyes, gave a quirky twist to my lips.

"'Twas fat, ugly." He began to unhitch the animals from the wagon. "Nice people. They kept loading more stuff on the wagon. Maybe you can use it," they said. "We don't need anything — just the truck."

Once, for kicks, my high school girl friend and I enrolled in an Agriculture and Animal Husbandry class. We were the only girls, but there were cute boys, most of them from the farm. Naturally, we were the "green horns," the butt of their jokes, teasing and ridicule. However, it was my husband, a handsome Western Trading Post manager, who taught me the difference between wheat, oats and barley, corn and maize. While out for a Sunday drive in the country, he stopped his car, crawled over the barbed wire fence and gathered dry heads of crops maturing in the field. He rolled the husk loosely in his hand, blew the chaff away and dropped kernels of golden grain into my hand. He explained their difference, how they grew, their use. Then he planted a few kisses. Wow. If we had field trips like that with the high school class, all of us would have been straight A students. . . .

Looking at this assortment, LIVESTOCK and FARM MACHINERY became two black mules, named Jack and Joe, a gray mare who snubbed the mules and an unlikely companion, a pinto pony.

The mules, especially the one with the white circles around his eyes and mouth, looked scary to me. I had seen a few in my life.

I heard people say "he's stubborn as a mule;" a one-year-old child could "kick like a mule" when he protested a diaper change and a "sure-footed" mule was ideal for mountain travel. I was jittery and somewhat apprehensive about them.

As I walked near Jack, the one with big Al Jolson eyes, he twitched his thick upper lip and I thought he was going to sneeze. Instead, he raised his head and bared a row of yellowed teeth, which reminded me of Aunt Molly's old pump organ. He let out a raucous haw-w-w, he haw, he haw. It scared me silly, that unexpected outburst. I was almost reduced to an embarrassing state of infancy.

"What brought that on?" I asked.

"Aw, he was just trying to get acquainted."

"Well, I could have done with a less explosive introduction." Something told me there would be no love lost between that mule and myself.

FARM IMPLEMENTS was the long line of odd-looking machinery, which Bob tried to explain to me. There was a wheat drill, a riding plow, a bean and corn planter, a bean vine cutter with wicked looking blades, a disk harrow, and, among a conglomeration of other things, a three-section drag harrow, which was responsible for scratching the sun-dried road to raise dust to leave a banner trailing the procession as it arrived.

The wagon was filled to over-flowing with stuff — harness, pitch forks, wire stretchers, a post hole digger, shovels, hoes, garden rakes, harness repair kit, red salve for man or beast, folded burlap bags, machine oil, axle grease, a cream can, a two-gallon brown jug, a five gallon crock, sacks of corn and bean seed. Heaven knows what was under the brown tarp in the bottom of the wagon. I didn't wait to see.

"Everything I need. I could start farming tomorrow," Bob told me.

"What would you do if that generous man appeared at our door tomorrow and said: Mister, you take my wife or the deal's off?" That was my parting shot as I started for the house.

Bob shook his head and laughed. "You never know when to quit, do you?"

I have to hand it to him in a whopping measure. He was lucky — almost as much as he was my sweet, good-looking husband.

Gathering in Springtime

I thought the spring of 1933 would never come.

At last, every mud puddle from melting snow dried. The below-zero days when my husband's long underwear, retrieved in frozen effigy from the clothesline in the yard, no longer appeared like Ichabod Crane's headless horseman as it hung on the wall to thaw and dry. The children's Dentons folded at waist-line and hung over the back of chairs reminded me of my little boys warming their cold bottom by the open oven door after a romp in the snow .

The inevitable pan of snow melted on the far right side of the range. Without that precious soft water, there would neither be shampoo nor pinto beans that did not rattle on the plate after hours of high-altitude cooking.

Early darkness, long winter nights, dreary days coupled with four lively children in three rooms, suggested an attempt to walk through a cattle drive.

Standing alone on the porch in the early morning, I thought: This is my quiet time, my free undisturbed time when I can make my own appraisal of this farm and our life's purpose here.

A breeze as soft as Maude's colts' nose nuzzled my cheek. Not one cloud marred the splendor of the pink dawn as it blended with the fast-appearing blue sky. A feisty white Leghorn rooster came from the chicken house door I had opened. He strutted boldly, defiantly stiffened his floppy red comb and neck, crowed a warning to his adversaries. It was he who held the keys to unlock the golden door of the sun. It was his undeniable privilege to announce it. His impatient harem waited for his inevitable ritual to end, then began to chuckle and scratch tidbits from the ground. The hens clucked to their babies, who came in a yellow rush to share and enjoy. Muffled snorts and the sound of stomping feet came from the barn where the horses waited impatiently to be fed and watered.

Suddenly, I was jarred from my reverie. My "pause in the day's occupation" had ended.

"Mother, I can't find my spelling book. I left it right here on the desk."

"Make Bobby give me my shoe."

"Donny, quit pulling my hair. You'll make me go bald headed like Uncle Dennis."

The speller was retrieved; the shoes returned to its owner; Jean's hair was saved from baldness — at least for that day with no guarantee thereafter.

When everything settled to a lull, I went to the kitchen to make breakfast. Bob came through the door with foam still popping bubbles on a bucket of milk. "We're going to have baby rabbits," he whispered to me.

"How do you know?"

"The doe made a nest last night in one corner of the hutch. She is pulling the soft hair from her chest to line it."

With his usual trip to feed the rabbits, Bobby discovered the nest overflowing with squirming bunnies. His face glowed with happiness, his voice was high pitched with joy and excitement. "Mother, my doe has —"

I put my finger to my lips — "sh-h-h-h," I hushed him. Let's keep it a secret for a day or two. It will give the new parents time to bond with their new family."

The intrigue appealed to him, made him feel important and trusted, although it was a difficult assignment for a proud little boy.

When the torturous secret could no longer be withheld, it was time for the announcement and baby viewing. Bob brought a basket with a heap of gray-blue fur into a warm kitchen. We oo-o-o-ed and ah-h-hed. Each of us given the opportunity to hold, touch gently and press tiny balls of fur to our cheek.

"They're sweet as a puppy," one of the girls commented and I knew it was THE ultimate appraisal from her heart. All of the children loved puppies.

Bob covered the basket with a towel. "The doe is dead. I don't know what happened."

Bobby became stoic. His face was white as paper. All of us were numb with the realization that 14 baby rabbits had no mother to feed and care for them. I saw tears welling in the children's eyes and ached with the thought their innocence had received a jarring jolt with the doe's death.

Bobby, with his usual quiet withheld emotions, needed to be alone.

"Son, why don't you see if you can find some green grass for your buck? I saw a bunch near the north foundation of the house."

I urged the saddened little group to continue their play while I tried to act busy with my daily routine. I heard a voice outside the window. It was Bobby pouring his little heart out in mourning for his dead pet.

"Oh-h-h, my doe. My poor-poor-r-r doe. I wish it had been me that died."

It would take a long time for this cruel and crushing blow to heal. But, everyone was helpful as we tried to feed the babies with a medicine dropper. Would warm cow's milk be as nourishing as the mother's milk? I pondered. After the children had gone to school, I spent the morning and well into the afternoon feeding rabbits, drop by drop, dribble by dribble.

How could I know how much food a tiny tummy would hold? They nursed and nursed at the dropper and were apparently as hungry as when I began to feed them. One by one, they died.

"How many are left?" the first question the children asked when they came from school each day. The time came when I had to draw my lips in a tight line and announce "none" to their eager questions I dreaded to answer. . . .

Bobby was begging to attend school, although his sixth birthday would not come until February of the next year. He was like a rodeo horse, eager but restrained, waiting for the starting gate to open. Caring for the chinchilla rabbit did not offer sufficient challenge for his inquisitive mind and boundless energy.

We consulted the teacher at the Rock Schoolhouse and expressed our son's desire to learn and be with other children.

"Our enrollment is down this year," Mr. Halderman told us. "Many families have been forced to leave the district because of the Depression. Let him come for a visit. We will take it from there."

So, the five-year-old boy supplied with pencil, tablet and lunch went to school with his sisters. . .

Without the clutter and clang of play things and the children's voices, the house was quiet — so quiet I heard the buzz of a fly trapped on a piece of fly-paper. I hoped to get a head start on my war with those pesky insects after last year's continuous battle. I blamed the contaminated grounds on the share-croppers neglect of the barns and corral for the onslaught of flies.

Donny would not let me out of his sight. He tugged at my apron strings, demanded attention, whined to be cuddled and rocked. I understood. Lonesome is an understatement, a puny comfort for a feeling of absolute abandonment.

Bob came into the kitchen. "Our woodpile is down to a few

sticks. I'm going to haul a load today."

It couldn't have happened at a better time. We were living in the manner of our grandparents and parents. Why not go a few more years before their time and become gatherers like the Indians?

"Donny and I will go with you."

Now that the truck was gone, the mules hitched to the wagon were ready and waiting. I fixed a quick lunch, filled two jugs— one with water, the other with milk— grabbed a blanket and we were on our way to a new experience for Donny and myself.

Bob selected a place near the edge of a deep canyon where dead cedar and pinon trees stood in phantom-like columns. Time had bleached them white, the smaller limbs had fallen away years ago. Sub-standard moisture and ensuing drought had caused great damage. Ravaged by strong wind and extreme cold, a few conifer trees had survived and were still green and producing cones for reseeding.

He tethered Jack and Joe in a spot where grass offerred a special treat for their grazing. Magpies let their black-and-white presence be known by flicking their scissor-shape tail as they flew from tree to tree. As they became more aggressive they displayed their anger at our intrusion of their territory with loud squawking shrieks, bold switches of their tail close to our head. Chipmunks took advantage of unguarded moments, scurried to stuff the coveted pinon nuts in their puffy cheeks.

Donny, filled with delight of his new-discovered playground, piled heaps of dry cones and scattered them with short-legged kicks. He threw rocks and fed the birds from grain snitched from the mules' feed. He coaxed antics from the clever chipmunks and giggled at their almost unbelievable response.

We ripped the sprawling dead trunks of timber from their root-mooring base. The sharp splintering, shattering sound echoed from the rim of the canyon's rock walls followed by a weakening echo cadence.

Wood gathering was having a devastating effect on my thirst, appetite and flabby protesting muscles, which were unaccustomed to hard labor.

"Hey, slave driver. My stomach struck 12 o'clock. Time for a break."

"Thirty minutes for unskilled laborers is customary. I might make an allowance in your case. You're doing such a good job." Bob wiped the perspiration from his face and threw his ax to the ground.

We spread our blanket underneath a tree and enjoyed a hearty lunch of biscuits and home-made sausage left from breakfast, an apple and pimento cheese spread on crackers. The cheese was made from a formula shared by a caring neighbor. Cottage cheese from sour milk curd and two added ingredients, butter and pimento from the store, made up the simple recipe.

Donny salvaged leftover crumbs to feed the chipmunks, while we cleared the blanket. The hard ground was little comfort for an aching back, but we relaxed and rested. Our small son, who often spurned the thought of a nap, gave up and came to join us. When he had succumbed to sound sleep, we slipped away to finish the load of wood.

When the wagon resembled a humongous porcupine with trunks and limbs protruding up and down, out and over the wagon's rim, the mules were hitched to the loaded transport. It required an extra boost to lift me over the wagon wheel to the high seat — I wondered if I would have to be hoisted from my bed in the morning. Bob handed Donny to me over the wagon wheel. I cuddled a tired and sleepy little adventurer in my arms as we jostled toward home.

I was reluctant to leave the woods. The air was crisp, cool, invigorating with earthy freshness spiked with the tantalizing fragrance of the aromatic cedar. What a shame the beautiful red cedar was not available to be made into hope chests to delight the heart of young girls dreaming of prince charmings and marriage. It was an offense to nature's beauty, a travesty for it to be burned, I was thinking.

We were content to forego conversation, but my mind was playing its usual roaming tricks. If I had one wish to be granted at that moment, I'd wish for a tree for our yard. Under its spreading branches the children could play safely and happily for hours and days; where my husband and I could lie in a hammock in the evening when the day's work was completed, watch moonbeams sift through the branches, tickle the leaves and coax a jiggle. We could count the stars. When did we ever do that where street lights near our Texas home obscured them? The North Star, the Big Dipper, Orion, the hunter, Pleiades, the Seven Sisters would become our friends again, our search for them a reassuring ritual long to be remembered.

It would be a small thing to ask with billions and billions of trees in the world. WAIT. . . . With that one wish we could have a river flowing through this barren, water-starved land. Or, artesian wells that would provide us with the means to grow trees, beautiful crops, orchards, encourage growth, transportation, build thriving towns, promote better education with libraries, entertainment, the blessings taken for granted before the Depression. Great opportunities are lost by poor judgment, selfish shallow thinking, I reasoned, and I erased it from my mind.

Would our children be prepared to meet the challenge of a changing baffling world? Were they making happy memories to recall, comfort and bless them in their old age? Time spent at the zoo and museums, merry-go-rounds and picnics in the park, visiting the State Fair in the fall — one special day at the Oklahoma State Fair, every detail as if it just happened, flashed into my mind as if it were yesterday.

The Flying Machine

"Everybody ready?"

Papa glanced at the gold pocket watch in his hand, closed it
with a snap, tucked it in his vest pocket. "It's streetcar time."

We four girls in our Sunday-best organdy and dimity
dresses, our hair braided and tied with taffeta ribbons, and my only
brother, Merle, fidgeting in his new knee breeches, waited for papa's
approval.

Nodding and smiling, he touched my sixteen-year-old
sister's arm.

"We're lucky, Margaret. This is a day you'll remember as long
as you live."

Mama never had to threaten to sew Margaret's sun bonnet
to her hair. "Young ladies aren't pretty with freckle-faces," she told
her. "She is the prettiest, the most lady-like," grandpa said of my big
sister. Papa agreed as he faced her now with pride and approval.

"In a minute," mama called from the bedroom.

In the sitting room where I waited patiently, I could see
mama tie the baby's bonnet, pat her diapered bottom and hand
her to my father, She grabbed the blanket, picnic basket and diaper
bag, hesitated one minute to glance in the hall mirror by the door.
She flicked the poppies on her Tuscan straw hat, tipped them
becomingly to one side, pinched her cheeks and smiled, apparently

pleased with the reflection.

"Let's go," she told papa.

It was Children's Day at the State Fair.

We shuffled our way from the entrance gate, through the crowd to the animal exhibits. Sleek horses — black, sorrel, huge spotted ones with shaggy feet and cute Shetland ponies that switched their tail, their red, white and blue ribbons dangling to disturb the pestering horse flies.

"What a fabulous saddle horse! Reminds me of the one I rode in the parade at the Ladies High School in Columbia, Missouri," mama remembered.

Papa favored the cows. "Those red steers are like the ones your grandfather fattened for the Chicago Livestock Market in the 1890s." He echoed mama's choice of the animals.

We kids straggled along — bored.

"When do we get ice cream, popcorn and soda pop?" Mabel asked.

"No ice cream this early. You'd be a sticky mess all day,"mama told her.

"Let's see the bunnies. The baby chicks," papa suggested.

He carried the baby and picnic basket, mama held Lucy's hand and clutched the diaper bag; Margaret carried the blanket and guided Mabel. At my father's insistence, my brother held my hand reluctantly as we followed the crowd to the next exhibit. What if some of his pals saw him holding a girl's hand? Oh boy! He would never hear the last of it.

Poultry wasn't much fun either. Floppy-comb hens cackled, feather-legged roosters crowed and made so much racket I could barely hear Mabel. "What did you say?" She repeated: "I saw a black hen lay an egg. Yuck."

"No more scrambled eggs for me," she announced, curling one nostril as she grasped her throat and pretended to gag.

We enjoyed the downy baby chickens, watched them "cheep-cheep" and peck at the feeders, and each other.

"Aren't they cute?" Margaret poked her finger through the wire mesh to touch the soft cuddly rabbits. They twitched their nose like Aunt Molly does when she smells dandelions and gets hay fever.

"Come see the baby pigs," Merle called.

As fast as we could, we edged our way around big pens of smelly fat hogs. "They're as big as rhinoceros," papa commented as he held his fist to close his right nostril.

A white mama pig with a pink belly lay on a bed of straw and snoozed while ten energetic babies played near her. They squeaked, squealed, chased one another, routed through the straw and nudged their mother. She answered with a grunt as they darted around the pen like white butterflies. One bit the curly-cue tail of another and he squealed like a fire alarm.

Mama pig oink-oinked, turned over and the babies began a wild scramble, pushing, shoving, tumbling to her side.

"There's always one runt in the litter," mama remarked.

"Look at that spunky little boogher," papa urged, pointing to a runty pig. "He's climbing and shoving, determined to find a dinner button."

We were reluctant to leave the piggies. They were so much fun. Outside the building, papa bought popcorn and cotton candy. "Everybody shares," he reminded.

Mama took a pinch from my fluffy pink cone. "Might as well open your mouth and let the stars twinkle in it," she said with a smile.

Jellies, jams, pickles, pies and cakes had better appeal. "I'm hungry," Mabel said when she spied the cookies, rows and rows of them, some plain, some frosted, others decorated with sprinkles of chocolate.

"You were born hungry," papa told her. "I'll find the picnic area."

The lawn was covered with people laughing, chatting, calling to children as they flipped blankets, emptied baskets and spread their lunch. We sat on our blanket while mama nursed the baby. Papa and Margaret served us bread and butter sandwiches, fried chicken, bananas, purple grapes and mama's Sally Lunn cookies. From a nearby refreshment stand, papa bought a jug of lemonade and filled our eagerly-offered metal folding cups for the refreshing drinks.

"It's citric crystals and water," mama said and made a wry face. "A few slices of fresh lemon in the big glass jars make it look real."

"It's wet," papa said.

Refreshed, we began once more to wriggle, twist and squirm through the crowd. Soon we were packed like pork and beans in a tin can in the crush of the midway. Rows of sideshow tents, with fading colored pictures, lined one side. Concession stands with teddy bears, kewpie dolls, fringed sofa pillows and felt banners filled the other side.

"Step right up, folks. For ten cents see the greatest show on earth." A man dressed in black with a white shirt, black tie and a tall hat stood behind a flag-draped box and tried to make himself heard above the rumble of the crowd.

"He's a circus barker," papa whispered. He didn't bark once while we stood there. He kept saying: "See the fat lady of the Ozarks. The wild man from Borneo." A frightening roar came from inside the tent. "That's him, folks. He's as wild as a drunk buffalo.... Men, for twenty-five cents, see the man born in a woman's body."

A fuzzy-faced kid held up a quarter.

"Sorry, sonny, you'll have to eat more taters and gravy. It's for adults only."

I was intrigued with the pictures on the tents.

"That lady is so fat — I can't tell if she's sitting down or standing up," I told Margaret. A pretty lady in a fancy red dress and black ostrich plumes on her hat, had a mustache and smoked a cigar. A picture of a calf with two heads held me spellbound. Did he eat with both mouths at the same time? I wondered. Did he get a tummy ache with so much food?

"George, it's just a bunch of freaks, fakes and crooks trying to wheedle folks out of their hard-earned money. Let's move on."

She gave me a little push toward Margaret. Completely lost in the magic around me, I stumbled and bumped a big lady in a white middy suit and sailor hat — the same one who bumped me earlier.

"Tell the lady you're sorry," mother told me. I wanted to say to her: "She started it — bumped me first;" but I knew better.

Across from the sideshows, the concession stands with the kewpie dolls attracted us girls. A man attempted to throw balls into a basket but failed. The concession man shoved a kewpie into Lucy's arms and looked straight at papa.

"Three balls for a quarter, daddy. Toss them in a basket. Win a doll for your golden-haired little darling."

"Don't do it, George. That basket's rigged."

The man snatched the doll from my sister's arms. "Shame on you, lady. You made your precious little girl cry."

Mama shrugged her shoulders. She led the way with Lucy pulling back stubbornly on her arm, sniffling and whining with every step from the midway and the concession stand.

With an urge to look one more time at the two-headed calf's picture, I stopped. The barker man looked at me. "Little girl, get your papa to come in for ten cents. You can see the calf free." I fumbled for my brother's hand.

Where was my mama? Papa? Sisters? Brother? I had become wedged in the tangle of the midway crowd. All I could see was men's and ladies' clothes; none of them like mama's pongee blouse and linen skirt or papa's summer Palm Beach outfit.

Terrified, I began to cry.

I could hear the merry-go-round playing the "When You and

I Were Young Maggie" song; a hurdy-gurdy man with a red vest and a tassel on his hat twisted the crank on a music box while a monkey passed a tin cup through the crowd. I was no longer crying. I bawled real *loud* so my folks could hear me.

People stared.

I saw his blue suit with gold buttons and a tall round-top hat and billy stick. I knew what a policeman looked like.

"Where's your parents?" he asked me.

"I" — sob — "don't" — sob, sob — "know."

"What do they look like?"

"A man — and a lady with a baby. My sisters and brother, too."

"I'll take you to the lost kids' tent. Then I'll search for your folks." He led me to a huge tent where a bunch of kids were inside. Some were crying like me; others played contentedly with a collection of impressive toys. A nice lady in a white dress and white shoes sat with me and began to read a story. Still jerky when I cried, I said: "I don't want a story — *I want my mama and papa.*"

When I thought I'd about cried myself to death, I saw papa come into the tent.

"Pa-a-pa!" I shouted from the chair where I sat with the nice lady. I ran into his arms.

Soon we reached the benches where my family waited. My sisters gave me curious glances. From the corner of his mouth, Merle said: "Cry baby." Papa frowned at him, and shook his head. Mama spit on the corner of her handkerchief, wiped my smeared, tear-stained face and gave me a quick half-hug.

"NOW, we're off to see the Wright Brothers' flying machine," Papa announced. "AT LAST."

"George, it's twenty-five cents *each*. The little ones won't remember it. Take the two oldest. We'll wait here. The baby needs changing. Lucy is cranky and needs her nap."

"Mrs. Crawford," papa teased. "How many flying machines

have you seen lately? We'll all go."

Papa was like that. Always wanting us kids to see things — to do things so we could tell our grandkids someday. Once, mama told Margaret when papa wasn't listening: " Your father's hand slides in and out of his pocket like the lip on our syrup pitcher on pancake day. It makes me a penny pincher." Poor mama, she could not forget the hard times on the homestead.

"Are these all yours — or a picnic?" the ticket man asked.

"All ours and no picnic." Mother gave him a weary smile.

Inside the tent, two men, who looked like twins in blue serge suits and billcaps, talked and motioned to a strange machine that looked like my brother's box kite only it was *lots* bigger and turned on its side with two little wheels underneath it.

"There's the Wright Brothers," papa pointed to the two men who were almost smothered by the crowd. No one would find them if they got lost in the crowd. They looked exactly like most of the men at the Fair.

At the back of the tent papa found a wooden folding chair for mama. While he and Margaret stood in front of her, pretending to look at the flyer, mama diapered the baby.

"The brothers will be world famous," papa told us.

I didn't see any tall hats like Lincoln's; no ruffled shirt like George Washington wore in the pictures our teacher showed us at school.

If my brother was a man and would be famous some day in a big tent at the State Fair, mama would've ironed his pants real nice. She would have bought him a new bill cap, too, if his looked like it had been left on a chair and somebody sat on it.

"That machine looks like a gigantic dragon fly," my brother said after he and papa inspected it closely and asked questions of the brothers.

I first thought it looked like Merle's box kite. But those long things on the sides could be wings, the black tin tail — no rag tail with knots like my brother's kite — the tin nose sticking out in front and two paddles... How could it fly?

"Someday, we'll flit through the sky like birds," papa said.

Outside, I could hear the music of the merry-go-round, see the colored balloons, smell the popcorn, feel the chill of strawberry ice cream in my mouth, hear the blare of the carnival rides, savor the tickle of Jersey Cream pop soda on my tongue.

"Come on kids," papa said. "Let's have more fun. We have one half hour until streetcar time."

Snow

"The North sky is dark blue with threatening storm clouds," Bob, bundled head to toe in warm clothing, dumped an armload of fresh cut cedar and pinion wood in the wood box. "It's going to snow tonight."

We awoke the next morning to find our small world transformed into a picturesque winter wonderland. At intervals with an occasional glimpse of sunshine, chunky flakes of snow fluttered from the sky like fluffy feathers — so fast sometimes they obliterated the outside pictures.

The cellar, the rabbit hutch, odd-shaped farm implements, the stock tank and every free-standing object in sight was covered with snow that bordered on tedium in their numbers and identical snowy images. The corral fence sported snow saddles that challenged the children to come for a ride. Our lane flowed in an endless white banner with the dark top of the fence posts adding a decorative accent like picots on tatted lace.

The children were spell-bound with the intricate design of Jack Frost's painting on the windows. In their eagerness to make a peephole to view the magical transformation outside, they scratched away the lacy leaves and curly fronds of icy make-believe fern. "I can see the windmill. It's turning real slow," Bobby told Donny.

"Mother Nature is picking her snow geese," I told them as

they watched the flakes fall faster and faster.

"Goody-goody," the girls shouted. "No school tomorrow."

"Maybe for several days if the snow keeps up at this rate. I'm glad we filled the wood lot."

"We're not ready for this. I suppose we never are. But, the storm is here. We might as well enjoy being snowbound," I told my husband. "The temperature is dropping fast."

In the late afternoon, Bob again bundled himself in warm clothing to face the intensifying storm with the wind swirling over the humps and bumps to form snow drifts. It was his turn, not the children's, to gather eggs, feed the chickens and bring a basket of chips from the wood lot — if he could find them from under the snow. He took care of the livestock, fed and made them as comfortable as possible; brought fresh water from the well and tethered the whirling wheel to protect the windmill from the force of the wind.

The snow and bitter cold presented many problems on the outside, but life on the inside of our little house, almost lost in the enveloping whiteness of the world outside our door, was very much in the everyday pattern.

Snow melted in pans and buckets on the range for dish-washing, cooking, drinking, shampoos and baths. Frequent trips to the well were no longer possible. With strips of old sheets, we used kitchen knives to chink every crack, every keyhole to prevent the blowing snow from coming inside. At night, we heated laundry irons, and wrapped them in towels to place in the beds for warmth and comfort. Allowing for extras, those were the priorities as we learned to cope with life on the farm in winter.

"There's something magical about being snowbound," my father used to say. "Good people are in their homes; rogues are hunting the outdoors for warm hiding places."

In spite of the children's confinement and often a lack of

elbow room, the overflow of squabbles, laughter, giggles, teasing, periods of crying; the smell of home-baked bread, steaming pots of pinto beans and baked spare ribs created a homey blend of security and sweet peace from the woes of the outside world.

"Look! Here comes a truck," someone shouted, and we ran to the windows.

It happened so quickly, we were not aware of the exact time it occurred. The sun had popped out in a brilliance that dazzled our eyes as it danced sparkles on the snowdrifts.

A truck, in an attempted delivery of food and supplies to the country store, growled and roared as it punched its way down the lane, made deep cuts for the high-school bus to follow. The mailman's car was sandwiched between the two vehicles.

"I'll get the mail," I volunteered quickly, leaving no time for my husband's offer to do it.

I was anxious to escape the hubbub of the previous days. A sudden urge swept over me to once again experience the childhood joy of stomping through the unmarred drifts, to hear the squeak of my overshoes on the packed snow.

"Whew!" The smell of the truck's exhaust seemed foreign and unrelated in every aspect to the pristine beauty around me. However, I didn't let it make an excuse for me not to go outside. I shoveled the snow from the porch, looked at the distance to the yard gate and decided manpower was needed to clear the drift on the route. When I could no longer appear to have a legitimate reason for remaining in the cold, I went inside.

Not wanting to exhibit the effects of the cold by drawing attention to my red face, pinched nose and watery eyes, I looked away from the mirror on the wall, removed my coat, cap and gloves and blew on my numb fingers.

"Any mail?" Bob looked up from the heater, where he kept busy jamming a big log into its gaping mouth.

"Yeah. A letter from my sister." My stiff smarting fingers were having difficulty with the flap of the envelope.

I read from the letter: Did you know it was 35 degrees below zero last night? Coldest on record for this time of the year. I worried the kids would get uncovered in the night. You aren't accustomed to this kind of weather, you know. People have frozen to death in their bed in the past.

"Good grief! If she had children. she'd know we wouldn't let ours freeze to death in bed. I knew it was plenty cold when I spilled ashes on the floor this morning. As I swished the wet mop across the linoleum floor shards of ice formed."

A cold chill tingled my spine. I shivered.

The below-zero weather remained slow in making its departure. At noon, although there was sunshine, the temperature did not reach higher than 10 below zero all day. On the west side of the house, the afternoon sun had generated enough heat to melt some snow on the uninsulated roof. Drip, drip, drip. Drop by drop, by 4 o'clock the drops had frozen and formed three-foot icicles. Whoops of excitement, fascination and curiosity came from the children when they discovered them.

"Daddy, please, please, bring one in the house." It didn't take much coaxing. They touched it, tasted it, smelled it, lifted it to test its weight before Donny let it slip and fall to the floor and shatter.

The sunshine tricked some of the hens into thinking spring had come. They escaped from the chicken house, walked and flew over drifts to the barn.

"I'm afraid the chickens' combs are frozen. Those pigs, the little stinkers, got out of their shelter. Their curly tails are as dry and shriveled as old harness leather. Looks like we'll have rose-comb chickens and bob-tailed pigs."

Sure enough, the beautiful floppy red combs turned black and dropped off leaving only a trace of color. The twisted pig tails were lost in the litter of their pen.

Night covered us with a blanket of eiderdown softness. The snow-bound earth covered all of the man-made ugliness with a garment of unblemished white. A blue sky glowed; winking stars competed with rhinestones for brilliance.

Chores done. Supper over. Night-time on a winter night was the most fun of all. The walls rocked with the excitement of happy voices, laughing, squealing, sometimes shouting in their eagerness to be heard above the commotion.

"You've had them all day,"my husband told me. "Night-time is mine."

He bathed them, put them to bed when they were too young for games, indulged them relentlessly when they were older. He held the reins of the loving ring-master of the circus. He teased the children with tongue-twisters, nudged their imagination with flagrant descriptions, appealed to their understanding and alertness with provocative games. He never once complained or begged off as I often did. It became a tossup of whom enjoyed the evening more, the daddy or the children? He laughed so heartily, a childhood bout of asthma came back to provoke and leave him with wheezing and coughing. If I suggested a switch of games less hectic or to throttle the excitement, he stopped me.

"Children are little for such a short time, my dear." A sigh and cloud of sadness passed over his face for a moment.

Usually, I sat on the sidelines with a basket of socks and stockings to mend or a stack of clothing to repair after finding rips, splits, snags, missing buttons, three-cornered holes. My mother used to say: "It's a matter of robbing Peter to pay Paul" when I had to sacrifice one pair of stockings to make patches for others. With life in the wild west, the rough and tumble of play on the splintered boards of the closed cellar door, the rough bark of the fence poles, barbed wire fences and rusty nails, stocking knees disappeared faster than a mouse could chew a hole in a burlap bag of seed corn.

"Trot-trot horsey go to town to buy this girl a wedding gown," Bob sang as he bounced one of the girls on his knee. That proved to be the favorite game when the girls were scarcely old enough to sit upon his knee. As they grew older the rides became more rambunctious. The possibility of an imaginary cockle-burr hiding under the saddle or if the horse became skittish at the sight of a strange object on the road called a "Ford Coupe," a hazardous bucking took place.

"Daddy's horses are fun, fun, fun," they all agreed. His were real champions that could gallop, trot and buck tirelessly. The children grasped the hand reins offered, dug their heels into daddy's legs for stirrups as they squealed with forced terror and bounced, wobbled and giggled until dumped in favor of the next rider.

"Me next, me next," they shouted until each rider had his or her opportunity to tame a wild bronco.

Often, when their anxiety overwhelmed them as they waited for their turn, they came to me. They soon learned mother's stable consisted of two broken-down old nags who did pokey trots and expired after a couple of less-than-thrilling bucks. No fun here. I was left with my darning, mending and patching to watch the rodeo from my grandstand.

As they grew older, the games became more complex for the girls; the little boys had their own special songs and rides.

"When I was a little boy, I lived by myself. All the bread and cheese I saved I put on the shelf. The rats and the mice led me such a life, I had to go to London to find myself a wife. The streets were so wide and the lanes were so narrow, I had to bring her home in an old wheelbarrow."

A bumpy ride followed.

Out of his storehouse of childhood memories came an endless supply of "fun stuff." He gave playtime the enchantment of storybook magic. The girls trotted on imaginary ponies through tree-shaded lanes and daisy meadows to shop for a Cinderella wedding gown. With assimilated sounds, smells and pictures, he fed their imagination. The boys grunted and heaved as their daddy urged them to push the wheelbarrow harder through the cobblestone streets of foggy London. Sometimes in listening, I was carried away to make-believe-land myself.

"Let's play Bumble Buck now." This, an early request with no time to rest, gave the circus-master a few seconds to catch his breath.

My husband patted each child on the back in turn as he chanted:

"Bumble Bee, Bumble Bee Buck. How many fingers do I hold up?"

"Two," came Bobby's quick replay.

"Two, you said. Four it was."

The ritual continued until the correct number was guessed by each and the back-patting ended.

"Club fist next," June requested.

"OK. All fingers on the table. Come Donny, you can play, too."

"William Trembletoe catches hens. Puts them in pens. Some lay eggs, some none. Wire, briar, limberlock, three geese in a flock. One flew east, one flew west, one flew over the cuckoo's nest. The clock fell down, the mouse ran out. O-U-T spells out."

When every finger, except one, was eliminated, it came time to make a fist with the thumb extended upwards. The other children grasped the extended thumb, placed his fist in like manner until a pyramid of fists formed.

"Whatcha' got there?" my husband asked the player.

"A club fist."

"Take it off or I'll knock it off."

Donny considered the consequences and decided to remove his fist.

"Whatcha' got there?" he asked the last fist.

"Bread and cheese."

"Where's my share?"

"The rat got it."

"Where's the rat?"

"The cat got it."

"Where's the cat?"

"The hammer hit him."

"Where's the hammer?"

"Behind the church door cracking nuts. The first one who laughs or shows his teeth gets a blue box and a red button."

Eyes dancing, lips pressed tightly together, the children attempted to suppress laughter and smiles with no talking. Daddy made weird faces and noises to break their controlled expressions. When restraint became no longer possible, they broke the rule and received a kiss on the cheek or a pat on the bottom.

"Game's over. Bedtime," he announced with emphatic finality. "Last one in bed is a tar baby."

Shoes, stockings, socks and clothing began to fly in every direction as they scrambled to be the first in bed.

"Now I lay me down to sleep," prayers were said after which they received a good night kiss and a snug tuck-in with covers made with blocks of wool left from garment makeovers and lined with flannel fabric before we left our home in Texas; a blessing in anticipation of cold winters.

After the children's bedtime it was our time to cuddle together in the big Cogswell chair with our feet toasting on the matching stool by the fire to share our dreams, our plans, our worries.

Except for the plunk of a falling log in the heater now and then, the house was suddenly as quiet as the downdrift of the snow flakes against the windows.

Bob always grew pensive at times like this when we were first married. I wondered if he was reliving his experience overseas during World War I — the sea sickness on the ocean journey, the torment of home-sickness and loneliness, the fear of the unknown, the terror of battles, the sights, sounds and smells of the battlefields as he searched for the dead and the wounded.

He seldom spoke of those days now. Occasionally, I overheard names like Argonne Forest, Chateau Thierry, Alsace Lorraine and the Marne when a wartime buddy came to visit. Unlike many who returned home embittered with their emotions, bludgeoned and raw, he came back with the determination to heal, to do what he could, in an everyday way to make the world a better place.

I knew nothing of sacrifice. My emotions had never been tested. There remained much for me to learn to be an understanding wife and companion.

Too many times I brought my fears, doubts, dismay to those evening sessions, especially after the Depression and duststorms; the need to change our life pattern. The most important assurance was our vow to love each other forever, to stick together through thick and thin, to talk our worries over intelligently with respect for different opinions and to NEVER let the sun sink behind the Rocky Mountains with anger and hurt feelings in our heart.

"When the wolf howls at the door, sometimes love flies out of the window," he cautioned. "We're facing a ruthless enemy."

If I reached a place when I thought the world was about to collapse and crumble, or, like a meteor sending a shower of misfortune, he sensed it and quickly changed the subject.

"Bet you can't spell Winnipesaukee."

"W-I-N-I," I began to spell.

"Nope." He stopped me, changed the subject abruptly, which left the unspelled word dangling in the air as soon as I called an incorrect letter.

The word wasn't mentioned again for a long period; but it did pop up again when the going got rougher and tougher.

What in "thunderation" is Winnipesaukee anyway? I found myself, as my grandfather, talking to myself and using his pet words and phrases. It sounded like an Indian name. Maybe it was Hiawatha's grandfather's name. Or could it be the last name of the Indian maiden — the one in the story who died with a red-man's arrow in her heart and a white man's baby in her arms? Was it a rare wine? An exotic resort? A river? A city? A famous scientist? Who? What? Where? I had no books for research. They were somewhere in Texas. I dead-sure wasn't going to ask him any questions to expose my ignorance of the subject.

As the days, weeks and months passed, the incident was forgotten. I was too involved in the harrowing task of parenting, attempting to make-do with whatever was available amid trying to keep "mind, soul and body" together, as mother used to say during difficult times.

Then one day, a thought struck me, like a chunk of wood that accidentally flies into the air from the axe-blade. He was using that little spelling trick to divert my worry by changing the subject abruptly to something totally irrelevant. And each time as a result I began to recall a happy event of one of my father's Abraham Lincoln stories or to count each daily blessing and realize we were in good hands regardless of snowstorms, hailstorms, thunderstorms or another pregnancy during the Depression, which we couldn't afford now.

The worst blizzard of all came later. In early September, when the days were still sunny, cloudless and gaudy with its few autumn colors, two brothers, long-time friends of my husband, decided to take advantage of the good weather to make a trip to their ranch on the mesa. Cattle needed to be checked, calves branded, fences cleared of thistles, the line-shack stocked with provisions in the event a blizzard detained them in winter.

Their 5-year-old nephew begged to accompany them.

"He's so lost and lonely now that Billy Joe has started his

first year in school," his mother told them.

"Let's go, pardner," the uncles insisted. His mother buttoned Jim Bob in a light grey sweater and placed a red mitten in each pocket.

The truck moved cautiously through the one big gate for passage to the mesa, leaving the hazardous rock ledges and boulders behind them.

I imagined they unloaded supplies at the line shack. The busy day would have begun with Jim Bob at their heels asking constant questions in his little man-to-man talk with his uncles.

"Why does smoke go up sometimes and down sometimes?" The question might have gone unheeded.

They may not have noticed the sudden darkening of the sky and had no apparent warning of an approaching blizzard. They may have begun the long trek to the shack in the swirling, stinging, blinding blasts of snow, which would have whipped at their face and clothing as they struggled in an eerie white tunnel.

I can only guess that they tucked their chins deep to their chest, and stumbled along in a desperate effort to find the way to the shack. The uncles would have caught the little boy if he fell, correcting their own steps and struggling on and on with all the familiar places completely obliterated.. Obviously, they stomped through the September blizzard's freezing temperature and unknowingly walked through the big open gate, the only opening to the valley.

When the storm abated, neighbors and family came to the shack. It was then they realized the men had lost their way in the storm. They found them later that day, the frozen bodies of the men and little Jim Bob wedged head-first in the huge rocks below the rim of the mesa — one little red mitten clutched in the frozen hand of each man.

Doctor Bob

From the day our first child was born February 22, 1924, Bob assumed the role of family doctor. He became dispenser of orders to an inexperienced and sometimes reluctant nurse who was supposed to be living in my shoes.

In taking care of our children, he always knew where it hurt and what to do to make the pain better. Extremely sympathetic, gentle, patient, he possessed the rare quality of healing in the warm touch of his hands and fingers. He should have been a doctor. How many doctors could dispel anxiety and fear with a tender touch and a kiss on the forehead? His bedside manner was impeccable, the epitome of human kindness. He displayed the same qualities in treating animals on the farm as well as people.

Nursing was never my forte. I lacked confidence in my own ability to alleviate pain and suffering. "Too chicken" to touch a wound, I had to leave the room when a loose dangling tooth needed to be extracted. The sight of blood pitched me into near panic.

As much as I tried to emulate Dr. Bob's expertise, I bumped a bed, giving the patient a frightful shake, when I neared it. I pulled hair if I attempted to fluff a pillow and managed to dribble water in an eye as I applied a cool, wet bandage to a throbbing forehead. There is no doubt about it — I lacked the magic touch.

Bob did have some experience which I did not. During

World War I, his first duty with a hospital unit required the use of litters to pick up the wounded, dead and dying soldiers on the battlefield. He seldom spoke of those days; although, occasionally, I heard the words "Argonne Forest," "Chateau Thiery" and the "Marne" mentioned in the conversation with a visiting veteran buddy.

So, I became the "get-me" nurse. "Honey, please get me a warm blanket. A washcloth wrung out of cold water. A spoon for Castor Oil or Castoria, liniment for "growing pains" in little legs. A pan for up-chucking from a sick stomach. The list was endless. I fetched and emptied the potty and cleaned up the messes. Happy for him to take the responsibility, I relied on him, confident he knew what to do and would do it.

To tell the truth, I don't think he trusted me any way — not after that cold February night long ago when we were first married.

Bob had been complaining of an aching back. The injury occurred when he helped a neighbor unload some heavy machinery from a truck. We were getting ready for bed one night when —

"Will you please rub some of this on my back?" He held up a big bottle of WATKINS RED HOT LINIMENT for me to see.

He slipped his BVDs from his shoulders, slid them down below his waistline, then lay across the foot of our bed.

I pushed the flap of his underwear aside to expose a small hollow at the end of his spine. I removed the cork from the bottle, took a whiff of the breath-snatching stuff. "Whew! This stuff is potent. If it doesn't kill, it probably will cure." I tipped the bottle, poured a generous amount in the hollow of his back.

He didn't give me time to rub it in, but jumped up like I'd touched him with a red-hot poker. His BVDs fell to the floor. He began to hop and jig around the room, jarring the flimsy walls and windows of our apartment while he fanned his backside with his underwear flap.

I stood there bewildered. Why did he create such a fuss?

He asked me to do it. I began to wonder if his antics would turn to rage and if he would toss me outside in the cold with me pregnant, barefoot and in my nightgown.

"That stuff is as hot as blazes! I said RUB not POUR."

I thought I had followed his example, since I often questioned him about the amount of medication he used. "If a little will do a little good — a lot will work wonders," he told me.

After awhile, he quit jiggling and hopping around the room and explained the END result of my doctoring. We began to laugh like crazy until I had to lean against the wall to support my big belly with my arms. Suddenly, I felt water, a lot of water, running to the floor.

"Something's happened."

"Sure did. You laughed so hard at your husband's misery, you did a very childish trick."

"No! No!" I insisted. "It's something else. The book said, 'The water might break.' I had never heard of breaking water and had no idea what that meant — remember?"

At 6:30 the next morning, we summoned a neighbor to drive 15 miles for Dr. Seay, the country doctor. By mid-morning, our six-pound baby girl was born.

By noon, Bob was passing out cigars and candy as he bragged about his million-dollar baby as though, bachelor-like, he was totally responsible.

Remember me? I was there. Candy for me? I wanted sleep — a long quiet, undisturbed day.

In this pioneer country, we doctored by faith, patience, perseverance and managed to take good care of our children.

Childhood diseases — measles, chicken pox, whooping cough, bumps and bruises, cuts and scrapes — responded well to our old-fashioned remedies coupled with what was known as "horse sense."

We were stunned, numb from shock, left with a feeling

of utter helplessness when tragedy struck without warning. In a twinkle of a star, our community, shattered from its complacency to grim reality in a heart-breaking way, faced an unknown enemy with anguish and terror.

Early one morning, a neighbor knocked on our door.

"I came to tell you Browns' little boy died last night. At first, his folks thought it was just a tummy ache. He got worse. They decided to take him to the hospital in Trinidad. He died on the way. They turned around and returned to their home."

We stood there in shock – unbelieving, trying to make sense of what he told us.

"Mrs. Doak, one of the neighbors said you'd be glad to make some burial clothes. Mrs. Brown has some material."

"Of course, I'll be glad to do it."

The children were in school. We drove immediately to the Brown's home near the mesa.

While we were taking measurements for the burial garments, the 5-year-old brother clung to his mother's skirt, whimpering softly in demand for her attention.

"He's so upset," Mrs. Brown commented. "Can't understand what's going on."

Turning to the child, she led him to the sofa, covered him with a blanket. "Maybe he'll take a nap."

When we finished the measurements and collected the material, we were ready to return home. Mrs. Brown approached the couch to determine if her son lay sleeping. A horrific scream sent my heart to my throat.

"He's dead!" She staggered across the room, walking as though she struggled to climb stairs, clutching each chair and table for support.

"Something is terribly wrong here," I said to my husband.

Neighbors were beginning to arrive. "We must get her to

the hospital as fast as we can. The roads are so bad, I hope we can make it in time."

Trepidation and hopeful denial filled our heart as the possibility of bad news gripped us. We waited anxiously for a report from the hospital and the doctors on the case.

Finally, Bill Barnes returned from the county seat where he had gone for caskets for the two little boys' burial.

"She died." His voice had a noticeable quiver in it.

"It was something called botulism. A serum flown by a small plane from Denver left immediately. It came too late."

The hearse arrived late in the afternoon of the cold January day, after a long and strenuous drive over rutted roads frozen by below-zero weather. Mrs. Brown's casket stood beside those of her two sons in the little white church where a capacity crowd of old friends and neighbors gathered. Many stood shivering in the cold in the churchyard, unable to find room in the small church.

After a simple eulogy and a solo by a close friend, whose voice wavered with emotion, the procession moved outside toward the white-picket-fenced burial ground. Small headstones and wooden crosses stood in stark relief as we passed.

With the last gasp of the cold hazy winter day, the sun splashed a mist of gold on the mountain peaks to the west, cast deep blue shadows in the valley. The mesa became a shimmering ghost-like spectator. Crisp, spine-tingling air began to creep upward from the earth, sending shivers through our body with cold that increased our pressured emotions.

Mr. Brown, head bowed, shoulders sagging, moved slowly behind the caskets of his wife and two sons. A stifled, barely-audible sound of sympathy, love and caring escaped in unison from the throat of the people. He clutched the hand of his eight-year-old son, who had been at school when the fatal illness came to the other family members.

As the sun moved slowly toward the snow line on the peaks, the three caskets were lowered into the graves.

"They died of botulism. Tests at the hospital showed home-canned green beans or corn was responsible," Bill said. The rumor spread quickly, which caused a frenzied panic followed by a chain reaction of food disposal. Every household had canned beans, corn, beets and other garden vegetables — stashed away as a hedge against a hard winter, dwindling supplies of store-bought food and no money to replace it. The contaminated food must be destroyed. Every home harbored botulism, a dreaded new word that struck terror to the heart of everyone in the valley. We had no knowledge of the cause, the symptoms — the results of the poison. We did know Audrey and her two sons were dead. Until more could be learned, our family was obviously in jeopardy.

"I'll never again home-can vegetables. Think of the horrible risk we take with our children." I shuddered at the thought of it.

As I began to open the jars, I thought of the long hours spent in shucking, silking, plunging the ears of corn in boiling water, then immersing them in cold water. I remembered blistered fingers that cut the grain from the cob, hours spent snapping the beans and shelling the peas. Hours of washing and sterilizing jars in a hot, suffocating kitchen where the range poured heat and steam from hot water. It created an endless and exhausting project.

Bob and I emptied the jars into five gallon cans — 25 quarts of corn, 25 quarts of snapped tender green pinto beans and black-eyed "shellies," mature beans slipped from their shells. The golden kernels of corn, the plump green beans, mixed with snapped and shelled peas looked beautiful together in heaps. We were too frightened for reasoning or to have thoughts of what would replace the food. There would be no turning back. No regrets.

"I'll bury the stuff in the north field away from porcupines, coyotes and other animals scrounging for food." Bob loaded the big cans on a sled.

Other neighbors, more trusting, thought it was a horrendous waste of a good thing and decided to feed the canned vegetables to the chickens and pigs instead of burying it.

At the Collier home Sunday morning, the pigs and chickens feasted. After dinner, as usual, the entire family took a "Sabbath-rest" nap. Mr. Collier was the first to awaken. He slipped quietly from the house to place fresh cool water in the fountain for the chickens.

Dead white chickens dotted the farmyard. He ran to the pigs lot. Two fat sows, with their half-grown family in an adjoining pen, lay dead.

"Was it botulism?" With a horrified gasp, they added, "What if we had eaten those canned vegetables?"

They did not equivocate when their young daughter became ill one night and they had to drive 20 miles for the doctor.

"It was just an old-fashioned bellyache," Mr. Collier said later. "But the risk was too great. So, we dumped our jars, too."

Will we ever know for sure? The consensus of opinion accepted the fact that those pigs and chickens simply made gluttons of themselves due to the generosity of a confident and more trusting farmer.

Country Medicine

June, our first-born daughter, was the one in the family who could be depended upon to break the law of average. Wintertime brought the usual start of sore throats, runny noses, hacking coughs, ear infections, pink eye, whooping cough, measles and chicken pox to valley children — not June.

She awoke one muggy summer morning with an excruciatingly painful earache and sore throat. After we exhausted our mind's storehouse of every available home remedy with no relief, there was only one thing left — "I'll get the car ready. We'll take her to Dr. Woods in Kim."

While I went through the ritual of getting everyone dressed for the trip, I reflected on the name Kim. The early settlers had adopted a unique way of naming towns with the first letter of each home state of the group of farmers: "Kansus. Iway. Texizz. Oklahomie. Alabamer. Mizouri."

The letters K-I-M became the ones that garnered the most votes, Clever and fair, I thought.

When we arrived at his office, Dr. Woods made a cursory examination of June's throat.

"Those tonsils have to come out."

The worst drawback and fear in making our decision in moving to the farm was Bob's harboring a remembrance of his 4-year-old nephew's death from diphtheria. As a last-minute precaution before leaving our home in Texas, our school-age daughters were vaccinated for the dreaded disease. But, there was a lingering nightmare: What if the vaccination didn't take? What if the vaccine was old and ineffective?

Now, we were more skeptical than ever. We were thinking of letting Dr. Woods, an unlicensed-by-our-state doctor, operate on June. What a dilemma! We didn't have the money to hire someone to make the 100-mile trip to the county seat, where there were good doctors and a well-equipped and well-managed hospital. No money for hotel bills and meals. How could we ever be able to pay for the surgery much less the other expenditures?

We made inquiries in town and among our new neighbors about the doctor's credentials.

"He took our kids' tonsils out," one neighbor commented. "They did okay."

Her husband joined in the conversation, evidently to give credence to his wife's testimony.

"I'd trust him in everything. Besides, no hungry man is going to take time to ask what's in the stew — jack rabbit, prairie dog or whatever — if it's offered, and he's starving to death. A little framed piece of paper on the wall ain't no big help if you're sufferin'."

When the appointment date came, trying to conceal our anxiety and distrust, we went back to the Kim town-doctor again. He looked at our youngest daughter.

"This little one should have her tonsils out also. That way you won't be worrying about her getting diphtheria."

After a thoughtful hesitation, he said, "Tell you what. I'll take both girls' tonsils out for $25. You can pay me a little at a time. By the way, my home and hospital are on the mesa. I'm in town only on Monday and Friday."

With reluctance and unquieted apprehension on my part,

the deal was made.

The mesa trip proved to be more than we bargained for while we were in town. It was hot — too hot for early August. After a dry summer, the crooked winding road that snaked around huge boulders, ravines and chug holes appeared lost under a mantle of thick summer dust. Our old car jerked, bumped, sputtered, choked and stalled a couple of times. The three children in the back seat were quiet. Too frightened, I suspected, to complain when they bumped shoulders or fell over jostling one another. Donny, surprisingly, slept in my lap. He loved to be rocked in my wicker rocker with its lumpy cushion, and he was experiencing plenty of rocking from the motion of the bouncing car.

"What a blessed relief," I sighed, faint in heart, body and spirit. We struggled from the car to stretch our legs, thankful we had reached the top of the mesa in one piece. We gazed over the rim to the valley below. Except for a rare clump of trees, like a wart on a pig's back, the treeless land reminded me of Lizzie's biscuits — the ones that squat to rise and baked while they squatted — as I gazed at miles and miles of flat, uninviting, undesirable land.

We had no difficulty in finding the doctor's large new mansion with eye-popping elegance when compared to other native-stone houses. His cheerful wife and nurse, dressed in a white uniform, greeted us. But, where was the hospital?

"Nancy, our cook, housekeeper and jack-of-all-trades, will keep the little boys here. She'll fix lunch for them, show them the rabbits and goats, keep them busy and entertained. You can follow me." She moved toward her car in the driveway.

We found the small native-stone hospital hidden in a thick clump of pinon trees, a quarter of a mile from the house. We entered a small, sparsely-furnished waiting room with a quaint feeling of trespassing. When the doctor came into the room, he motioned toward a door after greeting us.

"The operating room and recuperating room are back here," and he disappeared with his wife.

We had agreed earlier that I would remain in the waiting room. Bob, who had served in a medical unit in France during World War I, became accustomed to being around hospitals full of wounded and dying soldiers. I had to admit I was too chicken-livered to be in the operating room and was happy that Bob would be there.

They took June first. Jean and I read the comics in "Cappers Weekly," until she found a doll among a stack of Kim County Record newspapers. Once I thought I heard June cry out in a gagging voice. I shuddered. It must be my imagination — my frazzled raw nerves. I tried to console myself that everything was progressing well in the operating room.

Time stretched like children yearning for Christmas before the doctor came into the waiting room. "She came through fine. No problems. She's asleep now for a nice rest." He took Jean's hand. "We'll go see your daddy," he told her. She looked so tiny, so trusting; it nearly broke my heart to watch her being led away like a pony being frisked away for castration.

I attempted to read the Kim County Record. (*Depression worse. Unemployment figures down. Government help slow in coming. Corn up, hogs down. Pinto beans — new low — four cents a pound. Cow and calf $16. Four pounds of 4X coffee 25 cents a pound. Three cans beans or corn 25 cents. Star Navy chewing tobacco 15 cents a plug at Churches Store. Valley News — Ames family had dinner with the Barnes family Thursday. Smith children baptized Sunday at the Rock School House. Matthew boy swallowed thimble, rushed to Dr. Woods in Kim. Mother sewing again.*)

Every word of it resembled a meaningless jumble. My head throbbed. I closed my eyes. I smelled antiseptics and felt ill.

"It's all over," I heard the far-away voice of my husband. He looked pale, obviously shaken but trying to hide it with a faint smile.

"The nurse will be in to show you the tonsils."

She brought two small trays. "These are June's," she pointed to two lumps of flesh-like tissue. "She will be happy they are gone. See, they are dark red, angry-looking and spongy."

"Here's Jean's." I couldn't believe it: Two tiny lumps no larger than the end of my little finger. They were healthy, unblemished, firm and as pink as the flowers on her dress.

Suddenly, I was infuriated. "Dr. Woods surely could see those tonsils were normal. They should never have been touched." Bob frowned at me and shook his head. The nurse left the room.

"Everything went well. It took less time than I expected," Dr. Woods explained when he came into the room. "I'd like for you folks to go to our house for two hours. You can rest. Maria will make you some lunch. My wife and I will remain here with the girls."

Mrs. Martinez ushered us into a large cozy kitchen where the warmth from a huge range helped to dispel my nervous chill. Surprisingly, after so much excitement, both boys took naps. We had to awaken them when Bob returned from one of his trips to check on the girls.

"Dr. Woods says we can go home. The girls are waking up. They will be okay," he assured me.

"So soon!" That road was precarious at any time. With the children in this condition, I could not imagine anything so absurd. It was too horrendous to contemplate.

"No need to worry," Dr. Woods assured us one more time. That was all — "no need to worry."

We put the boys in the front seat with daddy. I sat in the back with a daughter cradled in each arm, my feet pressed hard against the floor board in an attempt to cushion the shock of each bump and jiggle.

Now that Bob had traveled the road on the trip to the top, he was somewhat familiar with the chug holes and rough terrain. He drove slowly attempting to avoid the worst places and to make use of his brakes more often. At steep inclines, he pulled the emergency brake quickly to prevent a downhill run away.

We were hot, tired and exhausted when we reached home after what seemed like a trip across the Rockies in a covered wagon. We put the girls to bed, attempted to make them as comfortable as possible. Awake now, they begged for ice to cool their throbbing throat. Water from the well was warm and repulsive, even more distasteful now because of the high mineral content.

"Not to worry." Dr. Woods had given us no medication to ease the pain, no instruction if a hemorrhage occurred. No diet. No time table for getting out of bed. I suppose he gave us credit for having enough sense to know liquids would be required for awhile. When the girls felt like getting out of bed, they would do it on their own.

About 5:30, we heard Alex's wagon coming through our gate. He came into the house, breathless from walking fast and evident excitement.

"How's the girls?" he asked in a tip-toe voice.

"As well as can be expected," Bob told him. "It's so hot. That mesa trip was about as bad as it gets. We need a doc."

"Ice. Ice. Ice," June called in a muffled, groggy voice. "My throat hurts. Ice."

"What's she saying," Alex asked, his head cocked to one side to listen as deep concern etched the lines in his face.

"She's begging for ice. I tell you, Alex, it hurts parents to face the excruciating pain and suffering of their children when they can't do one thing about it. Somewhere there's ice, and we can't get it."

Alex shook his head sadly, listened again to the cries coming from the bedroom. "Well, I'd better go," he said.

It was almost dark when we heard a car sputtering in our driveway. We looked from the open door to see Alex parking his Model T Ford by the yard gate.

"Something's happened to Alex. Something's wrong. Heaven knows what."

He came to the door, a serious look on his face, as he entered the kitchen. Like home folks, he never used the front door. He carried a bundle wrapped in a gray and pink-striped bordered cotton blanket. Everyone in the valley had one — a Montgomery Wards special priced at $1.98. Handling the bundle as carefully as a sleeping infant, he placed it on the table.

We watched him unwrap a piece of ice no larger than my sewing box with the tole painting of a winter scene on it.

"Where did you get it?" we asked as one voice. A welcome sight. We couldn't have been happier had it been a 200-pound block and a refrigerator to contain it.

"I remembered the Kim drug store used to have ice cream once in awhile. I knew it would take ice to keep it, so I took a chance. Today's my lucky day. This was all they had until a trucker came from the city tonight.

"Well-l-l woman, I was bigger than that druggist. I was gonna have that little chunk of ice one way or the other.

"It's past milking time," he added on his way to the door.

Tailing Up

The silhouette moving steadily down our country lane had become a familiar sight. Early each Friday morning a team of well-fed, well-groomed horses pulled a farm wagon. The sun flashed shards of silver from the riveted harness as the horses raised puffs of dust with each clop-clop of their feet.

There was Alex, our nearest neighbor located two miles east of our southeast corner, perched on the high spring seat, his broad shoulders swaying with the rumble of the wagon. Blue chambray shirt, bib overalls, a floppy straw hat on his head — an old bachelor and "good ole boy" as Bob often described him. He looked neither to the left nor to the right but focused his attention on the broad rumps of the black team and the usual willow basket of eggs jiggling on the seat besides him. We could see the glint of the metal cream can anchored behind him.

"Old bachelor" was not a term used to be disrespectful nor to be a sly dig in ridicule. It was simply a gentle, quick and folksy way to say, "no longer a spring chicken — and unmarried."

It was cream day at the country store; the one big day of the week when farmers and their families came to have their dairy cream tested, sell their chickens and eggs and to wait for their checks to buy groceries.

They came in wagons, trucks, pickups, jalopies, Model T's — any conceivable vehicle that would hold cream cans, kids, the pet dogs and a wife to hold the eggs on her lap to keep her eye on the lunch stashed out of the dog's reach just in case the Babcock tester man and his wife would be as slow again as molasses from a McGinty Jug in January.

The ladies, a homogeneous group in bright-colored calico and gingham dresses and stiffly starched sunbonnets sat in the shade of the cream station. They exchanged spicy bits of neighborhood gossip, crochet patterns, recipes, quilt blocks and patterns of their children's shirts and overalls. After lunch they watched the children play London Bridge and Ring-Around-The-Rosey. The asophoedia bags, tied with twine to make a necklace for the Smith children, flapped wildly as they skipped, circled and sang.

"Did you wear an asophoedia bag when you were young, Mrs. Smith?" someone asked.

"Sure did. That's why I make my kids wear 'em. Kept me from getting germs. I never caught anything."

"She caught poor old meek Ezra," Sarah, with a hand propped over her lips, whispered to Lizzie sitting beside her. "He was probably asphyxiated by the smelly stuff. Didn't revive 'til the ceremony was over."

The men usually played mumble peg with their pocket knives in the lot behind the store. When there was a sufficient number of men and boys to make teams, they played baseball across the road in the Barnes' pasture. They laughed, joked and hollered at times like a bunch of Comanches.

"Run Smitty. Don't run like a wounded jack rabbit." ..."Spit some tobacco juice in that glove, Joe."... "Hey, Dick, you must'a learned to bat with your mama's ironin' board." It was all in good fun. No offense taken by the ribbing; no mean-spirited or personal slaps intended.

"Cream checks ready," someone called out and they headed for the store. "Weda' won if I hadn't got my britches caught on that barbed wire fence." "Yeah, we coulda' won if balls were made as big as cantaloupes. Old Barney coulda' hit a few."

Alex's check, after the amount of butterfat was determined, was barely sufficient to buy his groceries. He milked less than a half dozen cows, low feeders but also low-milk producers, which made an expensive mechanical cream separator impractical, he told us. Each day he hand-skimmed the thick cream from the big crocks of milk, transferred it to his cream can ready for cream day at the store.

Bob had no desire to spend the rest of his life milking cows. We had only enough cream and milk for our own use.

Alex bought flour, sugar, coffee, oatmeal, matches, kerosene for his lamps and other staples. Seldom was there enough money left to buy a few gallons of gas for his "like new" Model T Ford. Other than for a funeral, a wedding or a real emergency his car was never taken from the plank-board garage.

"Howdy, folks," he greeted us one morning making his usual stop on his way home from grocery shopping. He clambered down from his perch on the wagon, gave an affectionate slap to the backside of a black mare and led the team to the corral gate post.

Bob met him half-way to the house.

"Just in time, Alex. My wife said dinner was almost ready. I had gone for a bucket of fresh water."

From the open door, I could hear their voices as I made last-minute preparations for our noon-day meal. After three years, I was accustomed to "drop-in visitors" at meal time.

My grandmother, who had gone west in the 1800s as a bride with a wagon train, gave me some valuable and unforgettable advice. I learned later it was an unwritten code of the west and ranch homes.

"Always be sure you have plenty of food every meal for the men in the woods. Houses are far apart. Storms unpredictable. Somewhere out there a weary traveler or lonesome cowboy can smell a home-cooked meal from a mile away."

I also learned these burly westerners had big appetites and could make hot biscuits disappear faster than a thresher devoured pinto bean vines.

The men washed up at the stand by the back door, combed their hair and took their places at the table.

After a sizable meal of canned roast beef and brown gravy, mashed potatoes, cabbage salad, hot biscuits, fresh churned butter and wild choke cherry jelly, Alex stood up, patted the bib of his overalls. A smidgen of his longjohns peeked from his shirt sleeve and at the neck of his open collar. No woman, "unless with soul so dead," would fail to appreciate the flour-white underwear. He once told me he made his own laundry soap and his well water was soft and minus the mineral deposits which plagued most well owners. But that represented the way of the wells in this high country — one good, four weak or bad bad out of every ten drilled, we heard.

"Well-l-l, woman. That was the finest meal I ever ate. I could cut that beef with my fork."

His face lit up in a broad tooth-less smile. Like an old weathered barn, time had extracted shingle after shingle until the entire roof disappeared. Alex's teeth suffered the same time-extraction. With a dentist 100 miles away, simply "keeping the timber wolves from his door," in depression time was the best he could do. He had learned there were worse things in the world than being toothless.

"Thank you, Alex, I'm glad you enjoyed your meal."

He wanted to know more about the roast beef. We told him we learned of the canning process from our county extension agent and booklets we received from the Agriculture Department of the government.

"Tell you what," he said, scratching his chin. "I've got a young heifer. Thought I'd keep her for a milk cow. She's got six tits. I won't have a six-tit cow on my place."

No one said teats. Well, maybe a cattle buyer from the city, or the county agent, or some knowing farmer, out of concern for ladies present who might be squeamish or easily offended, used the proper words when the occasion warranted.

"Planned to sell her," he continued. "She's nice and fat. Good beef. I'll give you half if you will can my half. I'll help."

Our canned meat supply was running low. It would be early fall before our animals would be prime beef for processing. I gave a quick glance at Bob, caught his eye, and in a second, as usual, he knew what I was thinking.

"Okay, it's a deal," my husband told him.

On the designated day, we drove to Alex's home. I had never been in his house but we had driven by many times. Impressed by the bachelor neatness of his small home, his barn and out buildings, I wondered about his house. Not one thing appeared untidy or out of place.

I was even more impressed when we entered his house - furnished simply, neat and well arranged. The bare floor, scrubbed to a new lumber luster, smelled like a fresh mowed meadow. Gleaming rows of glass fruit jars stood on a homemade kitchen table - washed, sterilized and turned mouth down on paper-white flour sack dish towels. A galvanized wash tub lined with towels held large chunks of beef ready for processing.

We enjoyed the day, and time passed quickly as we worked, talked and laughed. Large cuts of beef roasted in the big wood-heated oven. Steaks, sizzled in large iron skillets, would soon be in jars with added drippings for pan gravy. Cubes of beef for stew, soup and meat pies simmered slowly. Bob ground the tough cuts. They were seasoned with peppers from Alex's garden, chili powder, cumin, other pungent spices and salt to be added later to cooked pinto beans. The chili would be relished when the cold winter came, I thought.

Alex could not conceal his delight when the last packed jar from the pressure cooker was added to the long rows on the table.

"Golly, don't that look good? I'm going to be feasting like a king," he bragged as his toothless smile stretched wider and wider.

Every time we saw Alex after the canning, regardless of where we were, the subject of beef-canning came up in the conversation.

"Well-l-l, woman. That's the finest beef you could ever pop a lip over." He was never going to let us forget his appreciation of our work and his good luck in our acceptance of his generous offer.

Never would I be able to understand why he preferred to call me "woman" instead of Thelma or Mrs. Doak. I suppose he thought Thelma was being too familiar and my married name was too formal and cold. But Alex would always be Alex — a true and faithful friend.

Quite by coincidence, a few weeks later, he came by our place on one of his "howdy" visits. My sister, Mabel, and her friend, Mary, both midwestern school teachers, were visiting us during their vacation. We were ready to sit at the table for the dinner-time meal when Alex arrived.

"Come and join us, Alex," Bob invited.

Alex glanced at my sister and her friend and started to give trumped-up excuses.

"Aw, come on," Bob insisted and introduced our guests.

The usual chit chat — the absence of rain, the Depression, the girls' visit, more families leaving our valley. Then Alex told the story of the canned beef.

My husband kidded Alex, and extolled his prowess as a cook, housekeeper, grocery shopper, farmer and of his expertise in making furniture for his home.

After a lull in one of those unexplainable moments, the conversation suddenly shifted to marriage.

"Sounds like you are a good catch, Alex. Why don't you get married?" Mary asked.

Uh, oh, we had heard of Mary's saucy repartee — sometimes a wee bit risque, sometimes a big foot in her mouth.

Alex's head jerked up as he stiffened his neck and sat straight in his chair. It was obvious he was caught off-guard by Mary's brashness.

"Who'd I marry?"

"Well, there's Nellie," my husband volunteered. I could see old Nick putting mischief in his head.

"What? That skinny old maid! I'd have to tail her up every spring."

I signaled H-E-L-P when I caught Bob's eye. I had been in the same predicament once. I knew Mabel was consumed with curiosity but afraid to ask any questions.

"Excuse me, Alex," Bob said. "Maybe I better explain 'tailing up' to our city girls... After a bad winter when snow covers the ground for long periods, range cattle have to be fed. Cowboys take hayrack loads of hay and fodder pulled by horses and a barge to scatter food for the hungry animals. Sometimes a few cows become so weak from near starvation, they fall to the ground and need a lift to survive. If they can be 'tailed up,' fed and watered, they are soon able to follow the herd."

Holding my breathe occasionally, I watched Mary, expecting her to jump into Bob's story the way our new buff rooster jumps on a grasshopper or to make an embarrassing comment or ask — heavens knows what? Thank goodness the children were in school that day. Several times they repeated things they overheard which caused us some embarrassment.

Bob took a couple sips of the water from his glass and continued, uninterrupted.

"Two men get on either side of the animal, reach underneath her belly while another man grabs the cow's tail. The word 'heave' rings out. The tail is yanked upward. The men lift with all their strength until the animal gets on her front feet. That's 'tailing up.'"

I could tell Bob and Mabel's friend were in cahoots, not satisfied yet in their teasing. I was ready to save Alex from any more embarrassment.

"Why don't you get married, Mabel?" Mary asked my sister.

"I've never found a man I can afford to support," came her snappy reply with a cut-the-comedy look toward Bob.

Alex changed the subject after an awkward silence. "Looks like it might rain. I'd better mosey on home," he said as we left the table.

A week later Bob brought the mail from our big metal box on the gate post.

"A letter for you, Mabel," he announced.

"It has a local postmark. Who would be writing to me?"

"Well, you could open it and see," Bob told her. She opened the letter and began to read it to us:

"Dear Miss. Mabel: I don't eat much. A little oatmeal for breakfast. Some potatoes, meat and gravy for dinner. Most of the time I have bread and milk for supper... I can't write any more today. I've been feeling poorly. I may have a touch of 'potamaine' poison. Alex."

Mabel, Mary and I whooped and hollered with laughter. We immediately received a scolding after we kept repeating "pot-a-maine."

"You girls should be ashamed of yourselves. That poor guy is dead serious. Besides, that touch of ptomaine could be disastrous. You school teachers are making a mare's nest out of a pumpkin shell over his misspelling of ptomaine."

Silence. For a few minutes.

"Come to think of it, Mabel, you can't get bit in the deal. Gummed, maybe," I said. We all laughed and that was the end of it.

Later, Mabel said she answered his letter. What she had to say remained her secret.

The Dream House

"I don't care who told you. He's either pulling your leg or he's the biggest fibber this side of Pike's Peak."

"Honestly, I give you my word. It is true. I can buy lumber, doors, windows, hardware, even nails, enough to build a nice home for $11."

"Come on, Bob, e-e-eleven dollars." I shook my head, wrinkled my nose. I wasn't going to fall for a corny joke like that. Surprised and somewhat dismayed that he would play with my emotions, I knew how desperately my heart ached for a home — the dream home we had planned for so long.

"I give up. What's the joke? The catch?"

"No joke. No catch," he assured me. "The coal mines are shutting down. Quitting business, maybe forever. Who knows? Electricity, diesel fuel and natural gas are replacing the need for coal to run the steel mills, trains, factories, transportation with trucks and buses and for heating homes. All of them are demanding faster, cleaner, more efficient energy to promote business as soon as the depression period is over. Great things are coming."

I listened. Sounds like windbag talk from the rumor mill in Washington, I'm thinking.

"You know how it is. It will take a couple of years, maybe more, for us to feel the effects of the greatness. Like the circles made in a lake when a rock is thrown into it — the circles slow and weaken at the outer edge. The recovery will not come overnight. Folks are pinning their hopes on our new president. Roosevelt's NRA and other programs before Congress have merit and deserve our support. Some will fall short of our expectations. Some of them may hurt. Remember, we voted for change."

"It isn't doing much for the coal mines."

"The coal mines have been hard hit by changing times and the Depression. Dismantling their company-owned homes and selling them will help others. Clearing the land will give them an option to move on to something better. A dollar per room is much better than letting the area become an eyesore, a blight on the community."

"How do we fit into the picture? Those homes are 100 miles from us."

"Several of us here in the valley have signed to buy homes. I did. One six-room and one five-room. The decision was so urgent there was no time to discuss it."

"What will happen to the people who lived there and worked in the mines? What about those poor blind mules that pulled the coal carts?"

"That is the unfortunate part, my dear. Many will move in with kinfolk in other states to wait out the Depression. Others will scatter to small towns and cities where they will blend into the new-found communities and compete for the few available jobs — start a new life. The children will go to school and be happy making new friends. You know kids — they may surmise something is wrong, but they also know their parents will eventually fix it."

"The blind mules that pulled the coal carts? What happens to them?"

"They probably will be sent to the soap factories."

I blinked. Felt tears gathering. "Those poor people homeless and jobless. They're being yanked from a simple, stable life and forced to struggle in a world that has gone completely upside-down.

There is talk-talk-talk and we are seeing few results. If it takes years for a recovery what will happen to us? Will we still be sitting here in three rooms waiting? For what?"

"This doesn't sound like you, Thelma. You're usually so upbeat about everything."

"Maybe it's because I'm beginning to feel weary trying to make fresh starts. The fire when we were first married. Losing our home in Texas —"

I looked at my husband, recognized the hurt on his face. He had expected me to be ecstatic over the chance for a new home. For the life of me, the only thing I could visualize was big piles of old trashy-looking lumber. I thought about it for a few minutes and began to bend a little for his sake.

"Perhaps this idea is so crazy it might work. How do we fit into the picture?" I asked for the second time.

"We plan to tear the houses down in sections. Haul them home on flatbed trucks."

We talked — a lot. The more I listened with my heart, I could see the possibilities and became interested, even somewhat enthused. Another home — not a three-room one. A large living room. A kitchen with built-in cabinets. A place to put things out of sight. A dining room. Three bedrooms — maybe four. A bathroom with lots of water after we drilled a new well.

I pictured the new home setting on the hill east of our present location. It wasn't a real hill, only a slight elevation rise which afforded an unobstructed view of the distant Rocky Mountain range. A cool blue in summer, a frigid, shivering cold when the peaks were snow-covered. Between our place and the flat-top mesas to the south, a flow of prairie land with plowed fields enclosed with endless barbed-wire fences.

"I'll write my folks. Right away. They will be happy for us. It will be worth another three-cent stamp this week to let them know."

By return mail, a letter came from my father.

"The Depression is getting worse here. Employment has hit rock bottom. I haven't had a contract since I finished the big home on Classen Boulevard in Oklahoma City. Your brother, Frank, hasn't had any work for weeks. They can move their belongings in with us. Save rent. We're coming there to build a house for you."

Incredible, unbelievable. Everything was happening so fast. "With a few good rains and snowfalls, we will be ahead of our estimates," Bob assured me.

"This can't last forever. Good times will come again. Prices for cattle, hogs, beans, corn, grain will come back and skyrocket. There will be so much demand for them."

My mind was going like our windmill wheel in a brisk breeze.

Completely swamped in a state of euphoria, I couldn't think of anything except our good fortune. Then it happened.

Not one sliver of an idea had entered my head about problems which had to be solved first.

How could we squeeze five more people into three rooms? My parents, my brother and his wife, Bernice, and their 14-month old baby boy. Where would they sleep? How could I stretch the bedding? I couldn't. Where would everyone sit? There were only six chairs — enough for our family. Where was that extra table leaf? I hadn't seen it since we moved. Big meals each day for 11 people. I didn't want to think about it. And laundry — mountains of it! Barrels of soft water to be hauled from the neighbor's spring. I didn't want to think of that, either. Maybe this was the premonition I experienced when I bargained to bring the washing machine, although there was no electricity. I thanked the good Lord for my tenacity in that decision. A gasoline motor stopped the tub and washboard drudgery.

With four days left before their arrival, common sense told me if I panicked. Well-l, forget it. That was out of the question, I told myself.

I could almost hear my dear departed grandfather give his opinion about the seemingly hopeless situation.

"I tell you, those folks were so crowded in that little house they couldn't cuss a cat without gathering hair in their teeth."

One thing for certain: Bernice was full of fun and laughter. It would be an interesting summer.

They arrived on Thursday. That big old car was jam-packed to the roof. The jump seats in the center were folded to the floor. Tool boxes. Saws and hammers. Squares and planes. Crow bars and nail bars, nail aprons and straw hats. Mother, bless her, recalled times on the homestead when she was caught in a similar predicament, and brought blankets and pillows.

With the help of the men we shoved, pushed, crammed, turned furniture sideways, upended boxes, scooted beds together until we made everything fit like a glove with two bandaged fingers. A steel-spring couch replaced boxes on the east side of the house. We used one of the two mattresses in the bedroom on a bed in the yard.

"Bernice, the baby and I will sleep outside," Frank announced. "It will be fun. Like camping out. We can count stars. Make faces at the man in the moon." So, it was settled at that moment....

"Let's go up the hill to see the lumber," I suggested, knowing my father was anxious. Actually, I was as nervous as a hen on a glass nest egg. Would he think we had gone slap-dab crazy? Neither of us knew anything about lumber or building. Would he think we had chosen the correct location? What if?

I recalled the day we made THAT decision. While we were talking about the ranch and dream home we would have some day, it happened.

"Our new well we are going to drill will be much stronger," Bob predicted. "We'll get a water-witch to locate it for us. I hear the driller will be in our area next spring."

"I'll bet I can witch for water. I've seen witchers do it. Looked easy,"I said.

Bob laughed. "You — a witch?"

"Let me try it," I begged.

To appease another one of my "goofy ideas," he obtained a two-and-one-half-foot willow branch, with two prongs that joined to form a facsimile of a chicken breast-bone.

I grasped both ends of the stick in my hands, began to walk slowly over the land with the pointed end directly in front of my body at a right angle to the ground.

Each time I came to a certain spot, having approached it from every direction, that stick twisted in my hands and the point bent toward the ground.

"You twisted it yourself."

"Honestly, I didn't. You try it."

The willow stick did not budge in his hands. He tried it again and again. "The well driller will be the one to decide the exact location," he offered in a conciliatory tone.

I'm not sure I convinced him or myself, for that matter, that my witching with a willow divining rod had any merit. Anyway, it made fun and laughter,although I never heard the last of my water witching experience.

No one said a word as my father looked over the huge piles of walls — sections with gaping holes where doors and windows were once installed.

"Looks like a large commercial building that has been completely demolished by a cyclone." My father shook his head and began a walk through the piled lumber.

I felt my heart take a quick slide like a spoon full of jello in my mouth. I held my breath for a few seconds waiting for his next words. I felt numb one minute, sick to my stomach the next. Could I be pregnant?"

We watched my father go from pile to pile as he turned boards to inspect the undersides. Sometimes he slapped a board with the palm of his hand, listened to the resonance. Another time he ran his hand over a smooth piece in a caressing manner to test its quality.

"This lumber is better than most of the material I'm getting at the yards these days. It's like kiln-dried — no warping. No splitting and splintering."

I took a deep breath, relaxed. I saw Bob do the same.

"You can't beat nature's way of seasoning forest products. It has been spanked by the wind of spring. Beaten by blizzards and sub-zero weather. Hot summer winds and sun have extracted the moisture after rains to toughen the natural fiber. It's good reliable lumber." He looked at me when he spoke again.

"Thelma, you'll be telling your grandkids about seeing Haley's Comet when you were a little girl. This house will last even longer than that."

Mother laughed. "Do you remember what you said when you saw the comet? It looks just like the picture on our box of carpet tacks."

Early Monday morning, the work began. My father was the foreman, the pinch-hitter, trouble-shooter and strength to keep the project from bogging down. He had an uncanny knack for bringing common sense to a dispute or controversy, calm and order out of chaos as he built homes, churches, commercial buildings and bridges.

Frank had earned his expertise and credentials at my father's side. At age 14, during summer vacations, he boarded the street car, lathing hatchet in hand, to nail lath on partition studs where plaster would be forced through the cracks to make the walls ready for priming, painting or wall papering.

Bob, having no experience in building, volunteered to be the "go-getter" or "fetch-it" man. When extra strength was needed, he always worked hard and diligently at the task.

"I hope your dad won't be disappointed in me," he confided. "I don't know a plumb bob from a Buster Brown hair bob."

"You'll do just fine," I assured him. "Dad is a great teacher and role model. Patient and understanding."

To me, dad was a miracle man, one who was ahead of the period in which he lived. Mother was a wonder woman. How could they have survived in a truculent, hungry world with eight children and sometimes an aged grandfather who lived with us. In difficult times, in good times, in success, in failures, they worked together as a team.

When a much-needed tool was unavailable, my father made his own — the bit to drill the homestead well; he invented a kaffir-corn header to cut the grain heads from the fodder; fashioned brooms for mother's use from the broom corn he grew; made mattresses from cotton grown on the homestead. At the end of a hard work day, he rode horseback to a small one-room schoolhouse, where he taught nightschool for illiterate farmers, some of whom signed their claim papers with an X, to read, to write and to estimate the amount of lumber needed for buildings required by the homestead laws.

After years of experience caring for his family and helping others, he lost his business in an attempt to help feed families of the 1910-to-1914 "hard times" with credit. Bills came due from the wholesale house. His files were bulging with hundreds of unpaid bills he could not refuse to honor when he saw the thin, emaciated appearance of the children of customers and friends.

His business was gone, lost to bankruptcy; he became

another unemployed statistic with a big family. When every hope for work was exhausted, he traveled by horse and buggy in winter weather, using hot bricks at his feet and a warm laprobe, to sell subscriptions to the Daily Oklahoman newspaper. Mother, as a practical nurse, assisted our family doctor in caring for the sick and suffering from poor diets and neglect. Margaret, my oldest sister, gave daytime care to the young siblings of the family.

The farm work demanded attention each day. It could not stand still and wait for the house to be built. Bob had to sandwich his time between the two projects.

Occasionally, my father and Frank left their work to assist him. When the meager pinto bean crop was ready for harvest, the three men joined the threshing crew. I had done some pinch-hitting to row the beans for drying in the sun last year and was happy for the added assistance at this time. As I recalled my aching back, I said, "Thank you," long and loud.

The days passed quickly. We were tired at night, went to bed early and slept like babies. There was no telephone, radio, car horns blaring, fire sirens screaming to disturb us. We awoke each morning rested, refreshed, ready to meet the new day.

We women had established a routine of sorts and managed to stay out of each other's way and to avoid calamities.

As much as I wished the children would sleep late, they were up with the first rooster crow, all of them demanding something at the same time. Shoes and clothing were lost in piles of bedding dumped from the outside bed. Donny darted around the room with his bare bottom mooning everyone and refused to let June, his sister, help him to get dressed.

It was a matter of nimbleness and dexterity as we side-swiped each other to avoid a collision with a steaming coffee pot, dodging a skillet of bacon drippings as we wove our way through the early morning traffic.

The men shared the morning chores. Frank and Bob milked the cows and fed the chickens. My father loved horses and took great delight in caring for and petting them. They came to the house with ravenous appetites for a big breakfast of bacon, eggs, hot biscuits and fresh-churned butter. When the choke cherry jelly and honey were gone, Dad came home from the country store one day with a gallon bucket of white Karo syrup.

"Gotta have sweets with those hot biscuits and butter." He winked his eye and made a clucking sound with his teeth.

With the dish washing done, we brought a semblance of order to the kitchen before we began the bed-making.

"Please find a place to play where you won't be run over or hit by a flying object," I cautioned the children.

"Look at that clock," mother exclaimed. "It's almost time to get dinner. We've hardly had time to catch a deep breath."

"What's on the menu?" I was ready to flop in the first chair I could find that wasn't loaded with STUFF, my definition for anything and everything unnecessary, unwanted, undesirable, worthless, sometimes detested and I couldn't live without it.

"Everyone goes for corn on the cob," Bernice suggested.

"We forgot to soak the pinto beans in soft water last night, so corn it is."

We grabbed an old basket from the cluttered back porch, swung it between us and headed for the cornfield.

I think my sister-in-law remembered every story she had heard in her entire life. She kept me laughing until I had difficulty yanking the green ears of corn from the stalks.

"Did you ever hear the story about the old lady who got mad at her parrot?"

"No. You'll have to save it for another time. My sides ache from laughing so much. Don't know if I'll make it back to the house. Let's go."

On days when Bernice appeared to be homesick or missing the company of her young married friends, she went for long walks with her husband to bring the cows from the pasture.

They were later than usual when they returned from the pasture one evening.

"I thought you got lost in the deep forest," I kidded her.

She looked puzzled for a moment, raised her eyebrows, frowned, then brightened suddenly.

"Oh, that. We made love in the cornfield."

My father was a strict time-keeper with a five-day work week schedule. That left Saturday afternoon for doing something special. My family of Midwesterners found interest and excitement in the everyday things in life we took for granted. We depended on the gifts of nature to help us entertain them when there was time away from work.

"Today, we're offering a trip to the canyon. Any takers?" Bob asked.

Acceptance was unanimous.

"First, I must go to the grist mill by the mesa to have yellow corn ground for cornmeal. The wheat I'm taking will be cracked for breakfast cereal."

"That thick cream we have on on the cereal isn't bad, either." Frank smiled at his wife.

By the time the men returned, we were ready to go. We entered the canyon at the rim, followed a narrow, sometimes-hazardous trail around boulders and rocky ledges. Taking the children was risky but each adult was responsible for the safety of a child. We descended cautiously.

As we reached the canyon floor, we were delighted to find the leaves on the trees were spring green, the tall grass waving in a gentle breeze. Moisture had been preserved by the protection of high rock walls to lend shade. Each time we walked single file around a huge boulder we caught our breath and marveled at the magnificent view and fragrance of the trees and shrubs.

The fear of wild animals was something I had been unable to conquer since coming to the wilderness areas of the west. Howling of coyotes and grey wolves gave me chills and nightmares.

"Be on the lookout. We may run into a cougar or wildcat basking in the sunshine," I warned.

"Not really — you're joking."

"It doesn't happen very often these days." Bob wanted no alarm at this point. "Too many people have encroached their habitat. They are moving into the deep canyons. If we did encounter a mountain lion, getting up that trail hurriedly with five children would be no picnic. No balm for aging knees, either."

My father and Frank were profoundly interested in the rock formations. We stopped to rest near a wall of earth and soft stones.

"That white streak between the rocks — think I'll have a look at it," my father announced as he scratched out a small piece, looked at it closely, crumbled it in the palm of his hand, then smelled it. "This could be bauxite, a material used in making aluminum."

"Look what I found," Bernice shouted. "This rock has gold in it." She thrust the rock into my father's hands.

It didn't take long for the builder-turned-assayer to give a quick assessment.

"It's fool's gold. In the early days of mining, the old prospectors were betrayed by it many times."

"Oh, heck. I was already trying to visualize what kind of new car I'd buy. Wouldn't have to wait for the Depression to end."

We had a good laugh at her expense. She laughed the loudest. Mother and I were more interested in trying to find choke cherry trees. Evidently, magpies and other birds had harvested the cherries earlier. We found a few dried ones scattered on the ground. It was too early for wild grapes. They ripened later in the fall.

"They're mostly seeds and skin," I explained. "Like the cherries, the juice for jelly is all they're good for."

"Here, Uncle Frank, I found a cherry." Jean handed it to him. He put it in his mouth. "Golly Moses, those things will pucker you up so tight you can't whistle for weeks." He made a wry face and shuddered.

"Guess what I've found?" My father's outstretched hands held small dark-green balls.

"What are they?" Bernice asked.

"Gooseberries. We grew them back in Illinois. It's my favorite kind of pie."

He led us to a thick patch of low-growing bushes. All of us, children included, began to pick the berries, savoring delicious pies to be made later. What we didn't know was — we picked dark-green berries which ripened later in the summer when they were two times as large and a watery-looking pale green color.

"It's time to go home," Bob told us.

We returned safely but tired after our long afternoon trek. The weather turned cool. We built a fire in the kitchen range. Bernice, wearing Bob's old discarded wool World War I jacket she had confiscated when she first arrived at the farm, came into the kitchen. Before arriving at the farm, she had no idea how cool the mountain air was at night and early morning. She presumed it was like the blistering summer heat of Oklahoma in the summertime. She brought thin sweaters, sleeveless dresses and nothing for the baby to wear, except cute sunsuits. Poor little fellow. His teeth were chattering before we retrieved a pair of my husband's worn-out winter long-john underwear to make him some warm undershirts.

No chair was available. When Bernice entered the kitchen, she looked around and spied an empty five-gallon lard can by the window. As she attempted to sit on it, the lid slipped and she fell backward into the can.

Head and shoulders above the rim, arms flailing in the air, she looked over her knees to see who was looking. Twisting, turniing, squiriming only complicated the situation as her posterior sank deeper into the depths of the tin cavern.

"Help! Help!" She caught the attention of all of us in a hurry.

It was quite a tussle. Frank was having no luck as the can kept slipping as she struggled. My father was trying to restrain his laughter as the rest of us were making no efforts to control ours. Wanting to help in the rescue, dad held the rim of the can while Frank extracted his canned wife.

By September, the last board was in its intended place, the last nail driven. The house with its extended rock foundation ready for the native stone veneer, a barn, a large chicken house with louvered windows to inhibit night-time predators, a toilet with a quarter-moon carved in the door and graduated seating, and a box for past-season mail order catalogues were completed. It was time for good byes, heart-felt tears of gratitude and praise, and good wishes for the Depression's softening and employment availability.

Strangers

Daily newspapers printed it upon my brain. The radio screamed it in my ears. Who could ever forget it?

Thoughts of that 1932 heinous crime, which occurred before we came to the farm, was still bone-chilling and fresh in my mind. Like a mother hen who keeps a wary eye on a maneuvering hawk in the sky, I watched my children play in the fenced yard as I slid the blue enameled gasoline iron over freshly laundered clothing. I wondered if ever I would recover from the jitters. "Can I feel assured that children will grow up in a safe world?" I asked myself.

"My wife is worrying herself sick since the Lindbergh baby was kidnapped," my husband told our doctor when he inquired about my health after the birth of our last baby.

"Tell her there's no need to worry. Only babies with rich parents are kidnapped." He laughed.

In other words — forget it is the way I interpreted the message. I didn't appreciate his comment. "Try telling that to millions of mothers all over the world, Doctor Donnell," I thought. We had been shocked into a state of suspicion and distrust. Our days are filled with anxiety and apprehension. We looked upon the meter man, the ice man and the Fuller Brush man as a threat, using their employment as a coverup for stalking. Our nights are nightmares of horrifying dreams; the lightest noise raced our heart, left us drained and weary in the morning to face another day of repetition.

We began to think of deranged women out there; women childless and barren who would risk everything to claim motherhood with a stolen baby. Copy-cat ransom-seekers grabbed newspaper stories for fresh ideas. Words like "kidnapping" and "infanticide" would not go away soon. I became startled by my own shadow in an unguarded moment.

Charles Lindbergh, a handsome daring impetuous young aviator, stunned the world with his non-stop solo flight across the Atlantic Ocean. He smiled, a gleam in his eyes outlined by goggles, his white silk scarf waved a victory salute in his photograph, which was splashed across every newspaper and magazine in the civilized world.

"Lindy! Lindy!" opened a thunderous roar as he was given a hero's welcome upon his return to New York City. Ticker tape and confetti rained from the sky. Flags and handkerchiefs waved, the boom-boom of the drums in the parade could not muffle the tumultuous shout of the crowds.

Privacy was all they asked of the adoring public as he and his lovely wife, Anne Morrow, settled down in a pine-tree-sheltered suburban home. Here they could escape the tension of the pushy crowds, the constant media exposure, the request for public speeches and appearances. Here life was sweet and soothed by solitude and the whisper of pine trees.

One night, whether it was a cool breeze that wafted across his face or a slight noise, Lindbergh awakened suddenly. He went into the nursery where his 10-month old son lay sleeping. A breeze billowed the curtain over an open window, a ladder outside reached the sill. In panic, he ran to the baby's crib. It was empty. Who could ever forget a horrendous crime of that nature? I thought. The whole world mourned their loss....

I smelled the scorching fabric and realized I was standing there completely lost in my thoughts.

"Mother, mother! A lady is coming," the children shouted. I

glanced out of the window and saw a gaunt figure in a floppy dress approaching our house.

I turned the iron off and ushered the children into the house.

I saw her face, hardened by wrinkles like a leftover baked potato. Fate dealt her a hard life or she probably drank one for herself, I mused as she staggered to the door.

"Good morning."

She stared at me, and did not acknowledge my greeting.

"Ya gat some ga-a-s-s?" she asked, wallowing her words.

"No, I'm sorry."

She avoided my eyes, looked down at her feet, big and flat in worn shoes. I had a strange suspicion that woman might jerk off a wig and poke a gun in my face at any moment.

Then she acted as though an important something had almost escaped her as her fingers reached into the loose neck of her dress and adjusted a straying bra strap.

"Ya gat a ca-a-r-r wheel?" Her voice was nasally and whiny.

"Sorry, no car wheel," I answered. And I thought: "My fear is gone now. It's woman to woman and I'm the younger."

She made a slight move and I thought she was leaving. I kept wondering in my mind why had she stopped in the first place. What was her real motive?

"Could ya fix me a lil' lunch?" The words slouched from her lips.

She looked as though she had missed a few meals in her life. Since it was an unwritten code of the west — no hungry person or animal who came to your door asking for food was ever to be turned away. I knew what I must do.

The children, wide-eyed with curiosity, were with me. I knew in my heart, I had no right to judge this woman by her appearance, although I thought, if beauty came in a basket, hers certainly came up empty. I knew nothing about her or what circumstances had brought her begging to our door. She didn't look menacing. She was hungry, I had food. My fear seemed to have disappeared with the bra incident.

I opened the screen door, invited her to come with me to the kitchen. Her eyes swept over the room like a stiff broom. She showed no sign of emotion as she glanced at the children.

They watched me slice home-baked bread and roast beef left from supper the previous night. I wrapped a couple of big fat sandwiches in parchment butter paper, reached for a basket of apples brought from the orchards in the Arkansas River valley near La Junta, Colorado.

"More," she said, looking at the sandwiches. "Got grandkids out there." She nodded toward the country lane.

I looked out the window at the stripped-down car with a box-like contraption on the back. Grandchildren in THAT? I couldn't believe it.

When the loaf was finally reduced to a crusty heel, she appeared to be satisfied. She snatched the sack of sandwiches and apples, without one word and sauntered out the door.

The children went back to their play after we watched the car disappear from our sight. While putting my ironing board away, I heard tittering and giggling in the yard.

"Ya gat a car-r-r wheel?" my three-year-old was saying in an unbelievable mimic of the stranger's voice.

Encouraged by the amusement of his brother and sisters — not that he needed much encouragement — Donny wallowed his words as the stranger had spoken.

"Could ya fix me a lil' lunch?" The others laughed and giggled again. "You sound just like that funny lady," his sister insisted.

This was a new experience for them. Children learn fear. They are not born with it. With their limited vocabulary, everything beyond the norm or strange or noticeably different is labeled funny.

I was glad their sweet innocence was unbridled by the unpredictable brutality of life gone wrong, the fears and phobias of adulthood.

Later, we heard that the same woman came into the country store two miles from our home. She told the owner a sad story. Their daughter had died and left them to care for two grandchildren. They had no work, no food, no gas. They wanted to camp out and cut fence posts in the canyon for a few days. Her husband would tinker with the car and get it going so they could continue their trip to California.

It was a likely story and believably true of many who were forced to sacrifice their pride and ask for help during the Depression. Although the store owner had a heavy burden trying to help his long-time customers and friends to avoid bankruptcy, he listened tight-lipped and obviously was touched by her story. From his meager stock, he gave her what she requested — bacon, coffee, canned milk, flour and matches. He put five gallons of gasoline from his almost empty storage tank in their car, taking the risk of running out completely before a gasoline supply truck shipment arrived from the long trip from the small railroad town 50 miles away.

One week later they returned to the store. The woman shoved the bag of coffee, the kind packed in a paper bag with the opening rolled over a metal strip for closure, toward the store owner, who stood at the counter.

"Couldn't use it," she informed him. "Couldja trade for cigareets?"

"Food yes, cigarettes no," he told her.

She stalked out the door after giving him a mean look. Something prompted him to inspect the bag before putting it back on the shelf. After turning the metal strip, he poured the contents of the paper bag on the counter.

"Well, I'll be darned! Suckered by a nice old grandmother," he laughed. They had used the coffee, dried the grounds and put them back in the bag.

Although there were no telephones, rumors travel fast in a rural community. Stories of similar experiences began to circulate. The "poor old woman" would whip out a siphon from her pocket when there was no apparent way to obtain gas from a benefactor's car. The couple were fugitives, wanted by authorities in Texas and Oklahoma for gambling and fake credentials to obtain relief subsidies. Everywhere they traveled, they evoked sympathy and managed to slip through the grasp of local authorities.

The "grandchildren" of whom they spoke so pathetically were two half-starved greyhounds used for racing and betting.

Our minister at the Rock School House heard the stories.

"We have to accept the fact that there are mean people in the world today. They take advantage of a bad situation and kind-hearted generosity. They make their own laws. We have to be vigilant in times like this," he told us. "The Depression has changed us — the way we have to think and live."

One evening, our horses were cavorting playfully in the pasture. They teased their companions, kicked up their heels and nipped at their haunches. Chickens sat like feather balls, their head tucked under their wing. Pigs burrowed deep in the litter of their pen. Cattle hovered in fence corners.

All afternoon, the northern sky was as blue as Bob's new denim overalls. At first, a chill sliced the air; then a foreboding static-impregnated calm settled over the land.

Nature and the animals seemed to have common knowledge in being able to predict a coming storm, its time of approach, its duration and intensity unknown to humans. The sun was nearing the "greasy spot," as Lizzie used to say, the time when it slipped behind the Rockies quicker than we could say, "Franklin Delano Roosevelt."

When night comes, a family needs to be together — mother, daddy, children in their home. I never liked being alone in our old home when I was a child. To me, the silence was frightening. The old clock on the shelf in the kitchen ticked louder than usual; a sudden strike caused me to jump and squirm. If a breeze slammed a door, if the drip of a faucet sounded like the tap of a cane, I was out of the house in a hurry and did not return until my parents, my brother or sister, came home.

Here on the farm, the yapping of a lovesick coyote or howl of a Timber wolf would send icy fingers creeping up my spine. I knew I was safe in our home, but I had never quite quelled that childhood fear. Maybe my mother was frightened by a frenzied buffalo on her covered wagon trip to the homestead. Who knows? A childhood hangup can instill a fear that can last a lifetime.

I tried to make a two-fold bargain when the Depression forced us from our home in Texas to the Rocky Mountain farm.

For several reasons, I was reluctant to leave our cozy new home. To me, it appeared scary, remote, unpredictable and wild out there, but there was no alternative.

"I'll go if you promise me two things," I told my husband.

"What?" he asked.

"If you get a gasoline motor for my new Maytag washing machine and..."

He looked at me with a quizzical look, waiting.

"If you never leave me alone at night."

"OK, you'll get the motor, my dear." He hesitated a minute or two. "I can not promise the last part."

He looked sad, pressed his lips into a tight white line. "There is no way I can make a promise I can't keep. There will be blizzards, circumstances we never dream about, emergencies we can't avoid. Who knows? I promise I will do my best to avoid it. But to promise it will never happen — I can't."

After watching the animals, I knew a storm was coming, although it was only late September and unusually warm from the dry hot winds, the devastating lack of winter snow and spring rain.

It was sunny when Bob left early that morning. "Now, don't worry," he said. "I may be late, but I will be back."

All day I had been nursing a severe cold with laryngitis and an all-over ache.

I bundled myself in warm clothing to do what outdoor chores I could. I brought in the few pieces of cut wood and added it to the dwindling supply on the glass-enclosed back porch. I tossed bundles of feed and fodder to the horses and cows, and opened the gate to allow the calves in with their mothers. I had not learned the knack of extracting milk from the cow's udder yet and doubted I would ever learn. I also fed the pigs and chickens with the skimpy amount of grain available.

"It's getting cold," I told the children when I returned to the house. "The wind is starting to blow. We'll have to go to bed early. There is not enough wood to last until morning."

I looked from the window to watch the gathering storm. Two large wagons appeared in the lane, piled five-feet high with fresh-cut fence posts. No one in our area had such handsome Percheron horses and fine wagons. Who could they be?

It was not unusual to see post haulers those days. With the row crop failures and low production, pinto beans were selling for five cents a pound. Corn, wheat, hog, cattle prices were plummeting daily. Something had to be done to bolster the devastating shortfall.

A lucrative market for good fence posts existed in neighboring states and our area had plenty of white and red cedar in the canyons. It was rugged, back-breaking work that took muscle, brute strength and endurance to swing an axe; to face cold daylight to cook breakfast by a campfire and to sleep under the stars on 20-below-zero freezing nights.

The first wagon stopped near our entrance gate, then the second one. A dark figure clambered down from his high perch and walked toward our house.

"Please, quiet down," I told the children, who were playing in noisy confusion in the living room. "Someone is coming."

They ran to the window in time to hear a loud knock at the door. Absorbed in watching the men and the wagons, I was unprepared for the stinging swirl of snow in my face when I opened the door.

A huge bear-of-a-man bundled in heavy clothing stood framed by the doorway. Big brown eyes peered at me from a dark bewhiskered face that was almost covered with a fur cap and dangling ear muffs. He managed a hairy smile as he acknowledged my greeting.

"Ma'am, a bad storm is coming. We need a place to stay tonight. Our teams are tuckered." He smiled. "Guess we're pretty much in the same shape."

I was hoarse and chilled while doing chores, now my head began to pound. My tongue stuck to the roof of my mouth like butterscotch candy.

Why did they stop at our place? Probably because there were many vacant farm homes now. Neighbors had closed their homes, left to find work in the cities and southern cotton fields. Maybe it was because our new home was larger and appeared to them as one being better able to accommodate extra people.

What if the storm turned into one of those old-time terrifying blizzards and my husband couldn't get home? All of the harrowing stories I'd heard came back to me; the bargain I tried to make with Bob about leaving me alone at night. I couldn't tell them my husband wasn't at home. If I said he was sick in bed and didn't want to be disturbed, the man would say, "I'm sure he would understand if I could speak to him."

Like a far-flung lariat, my mind drew in every morbid story I ever heard about this wild area. I had to stay calm, to hide my fear and my trembling hand out of the children's sight.

I couldn't stand there forever like a pitchfork stuck upright in a haystack. So, I began to make excuses.

My voice came out in a nasal, stuffy-sounding nervous croak. "Our firewood is almost gone. I intended to give the children leftovers for supper and put them to bed early to save the heat.... I wouldn't want anyone to catch my bad cold..." I was making myself sound pathetic.

"I can see you're sick, ma'am. I'm sorry. We'll cut firewood. All you need. We're healthy. Not afraid of catching colds."

"All we ask, ma'am, is to let us stay out of the storm and give our horses a much-needed rest. We can do without supper."

My head throbbed. I felt the room sway. Every time I spoke, my throat felt like it was being stroked with my nutmeg grater.

The children huddled near me. Four pairs of eyes searched my face, shifted back and forth to the stranger, waiting for something to happen.

I knew the "Good Book" said when you help strangers you might be entertaining angels unaware. By no stretch of my imagination could I visualize anything faintly resembling angels in these huge shaggy-looking men standing in our doorway.

If they were up to some kind of meanness, how far could they get in a blizzard with four horses and two overloaded wagons? Where could they hide? What if I turned them away? If they were found later frozen to death in some ravine because they had become disoriented and lost in the blinding snow, could I live with thoughts of blame the remainder of my life? Similar storms had happened in the past to old timers.

In one misunderstanding moment, I don't know what triggered my urge to suddenly grab the reins of reality, dig in with my heels and attempt to curb my run-away fear of these two strangers.

"I have a little boy at home about your size," one of the men said to Bobby, who stood close by my side clutching my hand. "He has a pinto pony named Speckles."

I suppose that did it. I couldn't believe the high-pitched raspy voice that broke the silence belonged to me.

"There's feed and shelter in the barn for the horses."

He thanked me and left.

Soon we heard the crunch of the wagon wheels. Horses snorted, harnesses jangled as they were unhitched from the traces. Suddenly, a blast of wind struck the house, rattled the windows and sucked at the doors.

I knew Bob, familiar with winter storms, would not start for home in a blizzard. His homesteading days had taught him that. To think the children and I would be alone with two utter strangers made a galling chill sweep through my body and I shuddered. Why did I do it?

"Mother, you're getting cold," June, my oldest daughter, said. "Do you want a blanket?"

I assured her that I was okay. "Just a little tired," I told her, and we huddled closer on the sofa, waiting for something I could neither predict nor imagine.

We heard the loud thud of wood being piled on the porch. We waited. After what seemed like a long, long time, the men came inside. They coaxed the fading embers with kindling, then added wood to the fire in the living room heater. I could hear the clatter of stove caps as they rebuilt the dead fire in the range. In a few minutes, the entire house was enveloped in soothing comfort.

I lighted the lamps. In their gleam, the men resembled super giants as they began to remove their sheepskin-lined coats, fur caps and unbuckled wet overshoes and set them on the porch.

To my amazement, they were young men with strong

arms and shoulder muscles that rippled their flannel shirts. They introduced themselves: "I'm Jim. He's Andy." Their movement around the kitchen was quick, deliberate and graceful.

"What grade are you in? I have two girls. They're in the second and third grades." Andy, with the big brown eyes, chatted with the girls, who were becoming less tense, more interested.

I wondered how I could have been so terrified less than an hour ago when I was unable to distinguish the real from the unreal in my thoughts.

Their pinched features told me they were in need of some good hot coffee and food.

"I'll fix something to eat," I told them in a shakey half-whispered voice that bordered on an apology for being rude earlier.

"Ma'am, we don't want to trouble you none."

They didn't put up any convincing argument. With the house cozy and warm, my paralyzing fright abated; the strangers talked with the children, and I felt much better. In a few minutes, I had potatoes cooking, canned steak and gravy sizzling in the skillet, the left-overs warmed and coffee perking.

We ate supper, the children and I with the strangers. They spoke affectionately of their wives and children, and told us stories of their homes in neighboring Baca County.

When the meal was finished, they paid gracious compliments, thanked me humbly as they moved dirty dishes to the cabinet.

"We're used to this," Jim said. "I'll wash and he'll dry. We do lots of batching. You need to sit by the fire and rest."

While they were busy in the kitchen, I hurried to get the children ready for bed. By that time, I was more than ready to sit, close my eyes and try to untangle this dilemma. How and why did it happen?

Later, as they sat in the living room, relaxed by the warmth of the fire and food in their stomachs, they were nodding. After I tucked the children in their beds, I decided I would sit quietly and read the Cappers Weekly paper while they slept undisturbed in their chairs.

I could hear the wind whistle; the snow fell in large feathery flakes and piled up fast on the ground.

I read and reread the newspaper until I thought I could repeat the written material word for word. How could I sit here all night with these two strangers snoozing in their chair? I needed Vicks vapor rub, and a warm woolen cloth on my chest. I needed something to sooth my throat. I needed sleep.

I left the room quietly and put fresh linen on our bed in the bedroom. The heater door clanged as I attempted to add more wood to the fire. In a flash, they were wide awake and alert.

"I'm sorry. We didn't mean to go to sleep," Andy apologized. "I guess it was the fire and warmth and good food."

"I have a bed ready for you."

They thanked me and left for the assigned room.

As quickly as I could, I converted the living room sofa into a bed, rubbed Vicks on my chest, gargled and swallowed some cough syrup. I realized it would be a long, long night. Without removing my clothing or shoes, I lay down on the sofa bed in the living room with wide-awake determination not to fall asleep.

In spite of my brave effort, I did fall asleep. The rattle of the kitchen door sounded and I jumped to my feet. Were those men sneaking out the back door? Was I dreaming? What was going on? Something was happening here.

In panic, I ran to the children's room. They were still tucked in snugly and sleeping soundly. The wind had ceased. The snow had eased and the moon shed a bright streak across the floor.

In the dim light, I saw my husband. I rushed to him. Hoarse, tearful words tumbled out of my throat. I was near hysteria.

"These men — I couldn't —"

"It's OK, it's OK," he said, shaking his hands in front of me in an attempt to quiet, calm and comfort me. "I saw the wagons. I knew what had happened. The storm let up. A few roads were closed. I had to dig out a couple times when I missed the road near the church."

We were up early in the morning. The sky was blue. The brilliant sun brushed the snow, sprinkled sparkles like confetti on the drifts. The storm had abated, dumping only eight inches of dry snow on the ground.

While the strangers fed and harnessed their horses, Bob and I prepared breakfast. They visited with us, told us more of their post-hauling days as we ate breakfast together. Their praise and gratitude for our hospitality was boundless.

We watched the wagons, the horses still snorting white vapors as they drove through the big gate and disappeared from our sight.

"I was so scared."

"Yeah, I know. I'm sorry I wasn't here. But it was the right thing to do, my dear. I'm proud of you."

He drew me close, gave me a big hug and tender kiss and everything was normal again in our Rocky Mountain home.

Sick Cows

"It's the driest period on record," Grandpa Dixon complained. "Add no snow last winter, no rain this spring — that spells disaster."

`"Always rains in May — and the Fourth of July."

"Don't bet your boots on it. Your feet might get scorched in August."

Local farmers gathered in neighborly knots at the county store. They joked and placed bets on the prospects for rain. They speculated on the possibility of flash floods if a gully-washer came as in the old days when rain went on a rampage after prolonged drought.

"I'd better start building another Noah's ark," Alex joked.

"And I'll sell tickets for passage on it," Curtis, always the enterprising grocery store owner and opportunist, offered his quick comment.

Days passed without rain.

It can't miss this time, we thought, as dark clouds scudded from the east to the south. Loud blasts of thunder ripped the stillness and rattled the fans in the windmill. A wild flash of lightning thunder cracked., and we wondered if an animal near a barbed-wire fence had been struck.

Nature teased with wide stretches of ghost rain clouds that

disappeared as quickly as snowflakes on a truck's hot hood. Sky rain, as mysterious and haunting as mirages, looked promising, but the telltale light streak above the horizon foretold that moisture would evaporate before touching the ground without leaving one thimble full of rain....

A few sprinkles fell after one of nature's spectacular thunder and lightning melodramas. Muddy droplets danced on the dust and the air smelled fresh and invigorating.

"If you smell rain before it gits here — that's all your goin'na git. Just a smell," Mr. Dixon told us.

Our Watkins' products peddler was a traveling almanac, weather prognosticator, dispenser of folklore and home remedies. "There's many weather patterns," he told us. "Ghost rain, sky rains and no rain." Watching cloudless skies, discounting the smell of humus on damp ground after a light sprinkle became a part of our everyday life. Folklore and zany predictions came and left with his infrequent visits.

We shivered and endured the flash after flash of sheet lightning. We shuddered at the loud claps, the roll of thunder and waited for rain.

Finally, in May, a light rain did fall, as predicted. The valley folks were exhilarated with smiles everywhere. Back-slapping and good natured humor prevailed.

"I told you.... The drought is broken," the Watkins man bragged.

We discontinued our usual trips to the field to watch the progress of crops planted early. The moisture needed time to work its miracle.

Then, as grandpa used to say, "The weather turned hotter than a hen laying a goose egg."

Anxiety, concern and suspense nagged us. We could wait no longer for an inspection trip to the fields.

Squatting between the rows, Bob flicked the soil away with his fingers in search of seed, while I waited beyond the plowed areas.

"Hold out your hand," he said when he returned from a walk through the rows.

Into my outstretched hand he dropped bean and corn kernels. "Some are as dry as the day they were planted." Others with polliwog tails lay brown and shriveled in his hand. There had been sufficient rain to stir the dormant force of life, but, after sprouting, there was no moist energy to sustain them. The embryos had died.

I expected to see gloom written all over his face. All he said was: "There will be other springs."

If he had said: "Bet you can't spell Winnipesaukee," the tears I struggled to hold back would have burst out in an emotional deluge.

"It's too late now. There's no money for seed. Too chancey anyway. An early freeze would kill everything."

As the prospect for a good rain decreased, the velocity of the wind increased. It hop-scotched across the north field, whipped by our house, jumped the fence now clogged with Russian thistles from last year. It gathered dust and dirt to form a huge whirlwind that gyrated over the south field toward Alex's farm.

"Are we ever going to get a break?" I wondered as dust devils rendezvoused, increased in number and size as they whirled, danced, spun up and down the countryside. The pastures were overgrazed; grassroots were whipped bare. Farmers' worries turned into frustrating obsessions. Day after day more of the same punishment hounded us.

"I can't afford to truck alfalfa hay and cotton seed cake from the river valley. If we don't get help from the government — or from somewhere soon — we're goners," the farmers complained.

How weeds can grow and thrive while gardens and crops wither and die is a mystery to me. Almost overnight, after a heavy sprinkle, a lush growth of thistles sprang up in the barren fields.

The forceful drive of the wind dislodged thistles from the fences, tumbled them back and forth over the plowed land, scattered tiny seed, then covered them with brown soil from the duststorms.

Lured by the appearance of emerald green pastures, hungry cattle began to nibble at the growing tumbleweeds. Soon the fields and bar ditches along the lanes were carpeted with them. The cattle feasted.

Sometimes when a door is closed, a window of opportunity opens, I've heard. Who would imagine fields of obnoxious weeds could be a blessing?

Someone came up with the ingenious idea of making thistle hay.

"The thistles have enough nutrients for good food value," the county agriculture agent told the crowd of anxious farmers and ranchers gathered at the school house meeting.

"Besides, they have precious water stored in them. The important point is - they have to be cut and stacked while they are tender and succulent without the stickers. That is — before they are ready to mature."

A haying frenzy started. Neighbors helped neighbors. Men harvested. Women cooked food for the hard working men. Horses, wagons, barges, mowers, pitchforks, and muscle to do the job were assembled. Impressive loaf-like stacks began to appear in feed lots. Load after load of thistles were stacked, layer upon layer, with handsful of salt scattered upon them to tease and encourage the cows' appetite.

As the light moisture had encouraged the growth of thistles, the extreme drought caused prickly cactus to pop up in areas where none had grown previously. Ranchers discovered their cattle were exploring warily. They dispatched their cowboys with acetylene torches to burn the sharp spines from the broad leaves of the encroaching plants. After the torching, juicy, sticker-free cactus provided water made scarce by the lowered water tables and drying water holes in the canyons.

It was almost unbelievable. With the stimulating effects of the quick response to share in the common interest of all, neighbors appeared to be happier, spent less time worrying and complaining and more time praying for other miracles to happen.

With one problem solved for awhile, another one developed. The cattle cultivated a taste for the cactus. They became greedy and began to eat the untreated ones. Mouth and stomach filled with the fine prickles and dirt from the duststorms, they became sick. Other free-grazing cattle left their grazing ground to scrounge for tumbleweed thistles in the farmer's fallow fields.

"Cows are dying, eating too much cactus, too much thistle. They drink water, swell up and die while you're milking 'em," our neighbor warned. "I lost a cow and a calf just yesterday."

We had been fortunate. Bob had accumulated 18 head of cattle in a short period by bartering time, work, unwanted machinery, extra seed for row crops to help others. These are the beginning of the cattle ranch we will have some day," he told me with pride and enthusiasm. "These white-faced Hereford heifers are beauties. There will be more just like them."

"We're young and tough, but we have to face facts, my dear. No money crop this year. No money for cattle feed. We have to get help from somewhere."

"What about our feedlot full of hay?"

"Have you noticed how fast that hay is going? The cattle love that stuff. A head of starving range stock could tear our fences down and clean our feed lot in a short time. It's time to pay the Federal Land Bank — and our taxes."

"Maybe" — foolish thought. We had no rich aunts or uncles. Bob's folks were farmers struggling through hard times as we were. My father was a builder with few contracts in a crisis like this depression period.

"I'd hate to give up the heifers to pay taxes. Tomorrow I'll make a trip to see if I can borrow enough money to tide us over for awhile."

I dreaded the trip for him. It would be two days of chugging over bumpy, dusty, unpaved roads and one day to take care of business. Most of all, I hated to see the hurt pride on his face, which he was trying desperately to conceal from me. We had never borrowed money from the bank before to pay taxes or for anything.

After he left, I could not quell the uneasiness I felt. Perhaps it was the memory of my bargaining about the gasoline motor and being left alone at night. Who knows?...

"Let's get the chores done early while Donny is taking a late nap."

The girls gathered the eggs, filled the chip basket, scattered grain for the chickens. Bobby and I fed the pigs, threw a few of the remaining bundles of maize fodder to the horses; from the barrel in the yard, we filled the water bucket and range reservoir on the kitchen stove.

"The cows are coming home," I said as I watched them plodding homeward after a day of searching for tufts of grass in the dusty pasture.

Fourteen, fifteen, sixteen.... Two were missing.

"The white-faced heifers are missing. I have to find them. Stay in the house. I'll be back soon," I told the children as I slipped into my old leather jacket.

Our cattle had strayed once before. Bob found them near the abandoned homestead shack of a German man, who returned to his homeland to be with his comrades during World War I. He never returned. No one had claimed his property. The little wooden structure stood in sagging neglect and decay. Here would be the logical place to find the heifers, I reasoned. A plowed field bordered the half section of land on the east, which was now covered with tender green thistles.

I pulled my jacket collar closer to keep the cold wind from my chest. I walked faster and faster until I found the place where the heifers crossed over the Russian thistle and dirt-clogged fence. Their hooves had sunk deeply into the soft fine dirt, but left no tracks on the hard ground.

"Now what?" I said aloud.

Which way had they gone? The green thistles. of course. I should have thought of that instantly. I looked left. I looked right. In a low-land swag where the thistles would be the most lush, I saw two big turkey buzzards wheeling low, lazy figure eights. The bloated bodies of the red heifers made sharp contrast to the green field where they lay with stiff extended legs.

Numb from the chilly breeze, heartsick and weary, I returned home. The look on my face betrayed the results of my quest. I saw the somber questions in the children's eyes. I had to tell them.

The next evening, I heard the calves' loud bawl in the corral as they waited impatiently for their mothers. The cows should have been in the corral by now. I soon became more impatient than the calves. Where were they?

While I struggled with the twisted sleeve of my jacket, I saw the first group. The others lagged behind. Something was unreal in their stiff-legged, lumbering walk, I thought, as they ambled closer.

"Oh, no," I cried out in shock and disbelief. "They're bloated."

I felt dazed. Empty. Numb-struck.

"I'll go nutty if I take time to dwell on this." My heart was thumping like a mashed finger that had been caught in a car door.

Something had to be done. But what, for heaven's sake, could I do?

Mr. Bean. He was an old-timer who had been through

blizzard, droughts, sick farm animals. He would know what to do.

"I'm going to get help." I told the children. There was no time to explain. No time to quell their fears and anxiety. "Don't go outside. I'll be back soon."

I ran and ran the three-quarters of a mile. My throat became as dry as corn meal and twice as scratchy. Why did all of this have to happen with Bob away from home? In my wildest dream, I could never have thought of anything so crazy, so frustrating.

That familiar blue work shirt and curly white head leaning into a cow's side while he milked was a welcome sight.

"Our cows, Mr. Bean — they're bloated. Bob's gone to the county seat." Every word ripped at my dry throat, hammered at my throbbing head. "I need help. What can I do for them?"

"Nothing," he answered in a matter-of-fact tone. He looked up from the stool where he sat, still stripping the udder for the last drop of cream.

"Lots of folks are losing 'em. Sometimes they fall over dead while being milked."

"Surely, there's something."

"Sorry. I can't help you none. The folks have gone to the mesa doctor. Claudia's been sick again. I'm hobbling around. Hurt my foot." He stuck it out from beneath the cow to show me the clumsy bandage.

I stood there - motionless, speechless, waiting for my unwillingness to settle for defeat. To lose one cow would be disastrous.

"I've heard the last few days — some folks say kerosene and sody on a bridle bit — if you can get it in their mouth might help. If Bob were here, he could stick 'em. You can't."

I waited for the explanation of the soda and kerosene treatment. You're wasting my time, I decided, when he proceeded to tell me about the "stick 'em" instructions.

"Be careful," he called after me. "A cow could fall on you. Or one of the kids."

My knees were wobbly. I had to stop occasionally to catch my breath and rest. My curiosity overwhelmed me as I ran. I spread my left fingers wide, as Mr. Bean said to visualize in my mind a cow's hip bone. I should have been watching, not exploring mentally, a cow's backside.

I tripped. The road flew up and hit me in the face. The hard smack on my belly knocked the breath out of me. Humiliated, angry and hurting. something inside of me broke loose. I began to cry.

"I hate this bleak, colorless, punishing homestead," I cried out loud. I've had all I can take. I don't belong in a place like this. I've had enough flies, mud, blizzard, dust, dirt, gravel, cows, mules and pinto beans to last a lifetime. This is not the beautiful dream I had for my life. I'm working like a man. Doctoring sick cows, fighting dust storms, waiting for a miracle that won't happen." I pounded the ground with my fist, pouring out my pent-up anger.

I got up, put my hand to my back and groaned. My torn hose formed a ragged picture of two skinned and bleeding knees. My cap lay in the bar ditch. I swiped my jacket sleeve across my dirty face and dried my tears.

Slow down. Calm yourself, I lectured. This isn't the first time you've banged yourself. You know in your heart it won't be the last. You'll be doing things like this over and over again, until you're too old for anything except rocking grand babies, snapping green beans, shelling black-eyed peas and folding bath towels.

"Bobby, I need your help." Since he knew every animal by name, which cow belonged to which calf, I would have been helpless without him.

Calves bawled. Cows mooed. Bloated cows puffed and moaned creating a frustrating bedlam. A yearling escaped from the corral. Bobby chased it, yelling at every jump. A cluster of chickens, startled by my sudden appearance in the harness area of the barn in search of a bridle, squawked and scattered in a flurry of dust and smelly feathers.

If someone had asked my name at that moment, I would have answered, "Mrs. O'Leary," in spite of the fact no lantern nor fire was involved.

Thank goodness. Only a few of the cows had been raunchy and greedy enough to be in a serious condition, I reasoned. The unbloated ones were herded into the corral. Their hungry calves lunged at them, almost knocked them over in their haste to reach the mother's swollen udders.

"This one needs help, Bobby. She looks puffy."

I tied a rope around her neck, and handed the loose end to my son.

"Stand back as far as you can," I cautioned. "Keep the rope tight."

Before leaving the house, I had torn pieces of cloth and saturated them in kerosene. Into each I poured a mound of baking soda, tied them in four-inch rolls with string.

Now, with the medicated bit fastened to the bridle, I approached the cow.

It took ten seconds for me to learn that cow had no taste for soda and kerosene. It would mean a struggle — much more difficult than holding a twitch on the mule's nose while Bob pulled porcupine quills from his hind leg. As she backed away from me, I yanked the taut rope from Bobby's hands.

"Get on the fence. Wind the rope around the fence post," I yelled.

I gave a quick glance at the house. Three faces were pressed to the window glass, curious, watching, waiting.

The cow flipped and flopped her head. She yanked, pulled,

twisted and turned to avoid the bridle. Each time I held it over her head, she ducked underneath it.

"You cantankerous old bovine! If you had the sense of a grasshopper, you'd know I'm trying to help you."

I was almost ready to give up when the bridle slid over her head. I tried to force the bit into her mouth. She didn't have upper teeth, so I knew she couldn't bite me, although I knew she would if she could. That powerful tongue, so accustomed to wrapping around grass to snap blades from their roots, presented a forceful weapon. I had a feeling she might wrap it around my wrist and yank my hand off. I needed to stay on guard.

She was slinging slobbers and frothy slime, as repulsive as tobacco spit, all over me. I could feel a stream of kerosene and soda-drool slither down my sleeve toward my elbow. She slurped her slick tongue all over her frothy nose, mouth and chin and licked up the slobbers.

Suddenly, that cow swallowed real hard three or four times. She stopped and looked baffled. A loud belch reeking with the mingled odor of fermented kerosene and green thistle ensilage shook her body. It offended my nose. But Bobby and I gloried in it and shouted happily.

Glad I inherited my Irish grandfather's sense of humor and his ability to recall fitting and funny stories for every occasion? You bet. Many times it kept me from falling apart when I needed a boost at a crucial moment. It didn't fail me this time.

I thought of the old retired Quaker gentleman who, in his retirement, was learning to milk a cow. The cow showed her disapproval of his fumbling and pinching. To avoid another swish of her dirty tail across his face, he leaned to one side and upset his milking stool. Bossy kicked at him, missed her aim and sent the bucket rattling across the barn lot. Exasperated, the old man shouted, "I can't kick thee. I can't beat thee, but I can twist thy darn tail."

I chuckled to myself, felt somewhat relaxed for a few minutes. Bobby and I rested a bit and began to check the condition of the other cows. Most of them were now burping on their own; others were content to rest and chew their cud.

"It's too risky, son. This one is too sick for a struggle with the bridle bit. Get daddy's hunting knife with the long blade. It's in the left hand drawer of the kitchen cabinet."

I approached the puffy cow, slid my hand across her hip, feeling carefully for the hollow spot near the backbone as Mr. Bean instructed me. With my left hand on the hipbone, I spread my fingers wide like an open fan in an effort to obtain as much distance as a man's hand. My hands shook. Perspiration trickled down my neck and ran under the collar of my jacket. What if I murdered her? The thought staggered me. Would Bob ever forgive me for destroying his favorite animal for breeding and producing more of the coveted Herefords for our "someday ranch?"

"I forgot the tube we need. I'll get it," I told Bobby as I directed him to get back on the fence while I was gone. A minute or two away from the area would give me time to collect my thoughts, to settle down and attempt to deal with what was once an unthinkable procedure.

I cut a six-inch piece of tube from a hot water bottle hanging in the empty room planned for our lovely new bathroom — some day.

"We will be coming to the house soon," I assured Donny and the girls and I hurried back to the corral.

Once more, I located the hipbone, spread my fingers, located the strategic spot. Raising my arm, I gripped the knife with its long blade, pursed my lips, closed one eye and made a quick hard stab. A sound like the ripping of a taut piece of canvas followed the blow.

The cow didn't bellow. She didn't bawl with pain. She didn't fall over dead. She stood there, looking dumb-founded and puzzled. I examined the small hole. There wasn't one drop of blood, although I had expected it to spurt out like Old Faithful in Yellowstone.

Bobby left the fence and stood by my side as awestruck and amazed as I was — not convinced yet that everything was OK; we waited for sudden death by cardiac arrest or something worse to happen — I couldn't imagine what that could be.

Finally, I told Bobby, "Let's put the tube in the hole and see what happens next."

We didn't have to wait long. A blast like a whistling tea kettle broke on the evening air. We left the tube to do its work. We had done everything we could and not one cow had perished or was suffering any ill effects as far as we could tell. We removed the tube after returning the bridle to the barn, left the corral and returned to the window-watchers.

From my bed, I heard the kitchen door open and close softly. I had been awake for hours it seemed. I knew it was late.

"Is that you, Bob?"

"Who were you expecting?"

Maybe it was my imagination, but I detected a stilted bit of humor, so unlike what I expected.

"Please check the children. See if they're covered. It's cold tonight."

Later, he undressed, crawled into the warm bed beside me.

"I'm so glad you're home. We missed you terribly."

I cuddled close to share my warmth with my shivering husband.

He won't sleep a wink if I tell him about the cows — I won't sleep a wink if I don't. I keep the battle going in my mind. I had learned early in my marriage that the best time to break bad news or bring up something your husband might be reluctant to discuss should be after you were together in bed. He seemed to be relaxed and warm.

"Honey, everything happened while you were gone."

"Yeah-h-h," he answered sleepily.

"The cows got bloated." I didn't have the heart to tell about the heifers. Word tumbled over words, then they poured out.

He was so still, I wish he would interrupt me. Say something — anything to give me a clue to his thoughts. After what seemed like ages, he began to talk.

"I'm so sorry, my dear. I should have been here." His voice was low and hollow.

"You and Bobby did a brave but risky thing — so dangerous. Don't you know that all of the cows in the world would not have been worth two hoots in Guinea if something had happened to you or Bobby?"

Blinded by the urgent need to save those cows, I had never once thought of the possible consequences, the danger to our precious Bobby. I thought of Audrey and her two little boys. Quiet and remorse swamped me. I turned my face to the wall, tears fell on my pillow. I felt the three little I-love-you pats on my shoulder, but I didn't turn to my husband for the usual good night kiss.

Life can be so hard, I mused. Sometimes I felt I had spent the very last penny's worth of my heart, spirit and soul trying to make it through this devastating period of drought, blistering hot winds, duststorms and serious lack of water.

For some reason, a prickly feeling slithered over my body. A weird thought crossed my mind and refused to budge. Why did I feel I had been charged with childhood endangerment and found guilty? I'm sure Bob had no intentions of stirring up my emotions with his words. But something kept nagging me and I knew I would not sleep another wink all night. I began to question my values, my worth as a human being. The depression, the duststorms, raw exposed nerves, short tempers, provoked anger, unwanted blame forced friends to throw up their hands and say, "I've had it. I can't take it any more!"

I understood all of these things and promised myself to

work relentlessly to nourish our relationship and keep it healthy and thriving. I recalled the warning: "Sometime love will fly out of the window when the wolf comes in the door."

Like a loud clap of unexpected thunder — it came to me.

Bob didn't get the loan.

First Duststorm

I awoke with a nagging premonition — it had happened
to me before — something unusual was about to happen.
Uncomfortable with the strange feeling, I tried to squelch it as I
wobbled sleepily to the kitchen to make breakfast.

That Saturday was not unlike any other Saturday since we
came to the farm. To avoid a last-minute scramble in getting ready
for Sunday School and church at the Rock Schoolhouse, we always
made preparations ahead of time. "A stitch in time," had prevented
many disastrous situations in my lifetime.

My husband's scheduled duty was to clean and polish six
pair of shoes. With his World War I spit-and-polish experience, he
did it methodically; first he applied the black polish, rubbed it into
the leather, then gave the shoes a vigorous buffing with a woolen
cloth to restore a facsimile of the original luster. His specialty,
however, was shampoos, which he did amid the usual amount of
protests, sputtering and fussing by the children.

"Let June go first. I did last time."

"Daddy, you got soap in my eyes," June complained.

"If you'd stand still and quit scratching your leg, it would help."
He wiped the offending foam from his daughter's face. "Donny, go
pee-pee NOW. Don't wait until I'm ready to shampoo your hair."

"AND SO IT GOES," as Lizzie Reagan always said at the

close of her stories of life in the Ozarks.

I had my established routine interrupted often by unexpected and expected circumstances. After selecting suitable clothing for the six of us, I checked them carefully for missing buttons, soiled spots, possible rips, splits and tears. Special hand-washing at the last minute, pressing with irons heated on the stove required extra time. Lunch on Saturday was no different than lunch on Sunday, Friday or any week day. A full meal — no quick sandwich and glass of milk — followed by the regular clean-up job. The same routine repeated at dinner reminded me it was done in the same manner in my family home when I was a child. Some things never change. Old family traditions never die; they are reborn from generation to generation.

Before bedtime, a galvanized washtub was retrieved from the soft water barrel, where it served as a lid and deterrent for snooping animals, cattle and protection for the children who often played near the barrel.

"It was cold last night. Water in the barrel has a thin skim of ice," Bob announced as he set the bucket on the washstand in the kitchen.

From the range reservoir, I poured hot water into the galvanized tub and added cold water to ensure a comfortable bath. Giving a quick swish with my hand, I was satisfied it was ready for the first bather.

"Ou-ou-ouch! This water's scalding hot; I need some cold water," Jean yelled from the kitchen.

I peeked through the crack of the partially closed door. I saw Jean, squatted above the level of the water in the tub, looking as though she might suffer death by scalding at any minute.

"Will someone please get cool water for Jean?"

"My lap is full of stockings. I'm checking for holes."

"I will." Bobby volunteered. His response was almost

automatic, it came so quickly.

With pride and much satisfaction, I gave myself a mental pat on the back. At last, I was beginning to see results from trying to teach our children to be kind, helpful and thoughtful of each other. Suddenly, I felt sorry, even guilty, that I had often thought of giving up. Now, with that quick response, no prodding, no strict insistence, I realized I was doing the right thing and my effort only needed more time, more patience.

A piercing scream came from the kitchen. Now what?

Splat! The stockings were dumped to the floor as I rushed into the kitchen to see an impish grin fading from Bobby's face as he looked at an empty dipper in his hand.

"Bobby!" I made my voice harsh, threatening as I scolded him. "The next time put the cold water in the tub, NOT down your sister's back."

What's to be done with an offspring like that? The question popped into my mind. Then I recalled a recent conversation with my husband.

"Maybe it isn't a good idea for you to tell the children about your childhood escapades."

"Why not? I want them to know I was a normal, fun-loving kid; not one with curls, bows, white pinafore goody-goodiness like some mothers implied about their children." I'll admit I inherited my Irish grandfather's sense of humor. I teased and played tricks on my sisters and brothers much to mother's chagrin and downright frustration at times. Lack of adult wisdom and feeling, my teasing and jokes were sometimes warped and brought tears and hard feelings. I'm very sorry for that.

"Your chickens may come home to roost someday," my husband warned. I had work to do and was in no mood to listen to my mischievous childhood pranks being discussed.

I usually did extra house-cleaning on weekends. That

Saturday required special effort as I had invited the visiting minister and his pretty blond wife, Ruth, to have dinner with us after church. I also baked a cake, which was a rarity as I grew up in a home with natural gas for cooking and had not yet learned to bake with a wood-heated oven.

I baked. I crossed my fingers and waited. Would the dessert be chocolate pudding or cake again. I pondered.

What I served for dinner that day, I don't recall — probably southern fried chicken as that was my specialty. I often heard the words, "fried chicken and Methodist minister are synonymous," so I felt confident my menu would please my guests. . .

After Sunday dinner, the children took advantage of the unusually balmy day and played in the front yard. Ruth and I cleared the table, put leftovers away, washed and dried the dishes. I appreciated her help and was thankful for that acceptable practice in country farming. Cleaning up, with six family members and guests could be an afternoon's work, boring and condescending without help and conversation.

We joined our husbands in the living room where they were engaged in a heated discussion of yo-yoing cattle, corn and hay prices. The politics of the new administration and President Roosevelt's "New Deal" were being thrashed out in Congress.

"Whew! It's warm in here. Heat from the kitchen has engulfed the entire house," I announced, giving my forehead a quick brush with my forefinger.

"Let's go outside," Ruth suggested.

As we stepped through the door a blast of hot air, followed by a muggy calm, settled around us.

"It's more like the middle of August than the 14th of May."

"What in the world is that?" Bob suddenly directed our attention to the northern horizon.

A phantom-like scroll as eerie and mystifying as mirages

— and more frightening — rolled steadily toward us. Instead of diminishing in size, it continued to increase in height and strength as it advanced, rising higher and higher as it came closer and closer. The sky darkened. The sun was being almost obliterated by a thick swarthy haze. Warm air sucked at our lungs, making breathing more difficult in the high altitude.

Something impelled me to look away for a moment. A line of buff-colored chickens straggled lazily toward their roosting place at 3 o'clock in the afternoon. Maude whinnied to her young mule offspring and he bolted to her side. Joe and Jack stood near the barn. Their pointed ears stood up straight like gateposts as they focused their gaze ahead. The horses curtailed their afternoon frolic, assumed a sculptured stance, and waited in silence. Cows wandered clumsily toward home as they did each evening for calf-feeding and milking time.

"Maybe it's a forest fire," Mr. Rasmussen suggested. In the canyon to the north, thousands of conifer trees, cedar and pine, all highly inflammable with their high content of oil in the leaves and pitch in the trunks grew five miles away. In their dry condition, they could explode into a wild fire at any minute and spread quickly.

"It could be a prairie fire," another speculation Bob offered.

"The color isn't right," the minister said.

Unbidden, a scene from my childhood flashed into my mind. When my parents lived on their homestead in Oklahoma, I saw my father slumped on a chair, his clothing soaked in perspiration, his face covered with soot, dirt and anguish. A soggy blackened burlap bag lay on the floor beside him. Frightened and troubled by questions in my mind, I stared at his dark hair plastered in wet streaks on his forehead. I heard his tired hoarse voice telling my mother: "We licked the prairie fire this time. We may not be as lucky next time."

I sniffed the air and smelled dust. I could feel the erratic thumping of my heart. My lips were dry; my throat tightened.

Concerned for their safety, yet not wanting to alarm the children, I called to them.

Awe-struck and horrified, I felt some comfort in having the minister with us. At any minute I expected him to offer a prayer for our safety and the safety for all of the people in the valley. By shifting his stance from one foot to the other, he made me aware of his nervous state as he looked at his wife's ashen face.

"Come, Ruth, let's go before it gets worse."

He gave his Ford car a quick crank, revved the motor and they climbed inside the car and disappeared down the lane. A feeling of deliberate desertion overwhelmed me.

The house became as dark as a cellar when a flashlight fails. The air, thick with dust, mingled with a peculiar mustiness. We lighted the kerosene lamps and huddled together, speechless and numb with no clue what-so-ever what might occur any minute. The children, with questions on their faces, were assured they would be protected and safe.

The wait for the nameless terror was of short duration. A horrific blast shook the house. Doors banged shut. Windows rattled. The roof creaked. Every corner seemed to be shaken and wrenched loose from the walls. Flying objects struck with clamorous force and threatened to knock the house from its foundation and leave it in a shattered heap. The wind whistled, whined and howled like a pack of hungry timber wolves on a marauding prowl. From every tiny crack, face-powder fine dirt sifted into the room turning the lights into shimmering blobs of night-mareish haze.

We began to cough, sneeze, wheeze and choke. We covered our nose and mouth with our hands. We watched a brown straight line begin to form across the living room floor as the fierce wind forced dirt through the keyhole in the door.

Someday, I was thinking, the papers will say, "Many people were not frightened." If it's your house that's being shaken like a cat shakes a mouse, your nose and eyes and those of YOUR family clogged with dust until you can't see or breath — it's a different story. I'd be the first to admit I was scared silly and was ready to accept almost any concept of what might happen before we would see another morning — the end of the world, maybe.

"Looks like it will blow all night. The children are tired, scared and hungry. Let's fix something to eat," my husband suggested.

Every step stirred up a miniature dust storm as we prepared a snack in the messy dust-covered kitchen.

"This sandwich tastes like dust," Jean said after her first bite.

"Mine's gritty."

"There's brown fuzz on my milk," Donny insisted. He made an ugly face and stuck out his tongue.

"Better keep your mouth shut or your tongue will have fuzz on it," Bobby told his brother.

"I can't eat dirt — yuck." This from finicky June, who gagged once at the dinner table of a friend. I frowned at her and shook my head.

"Well, I ate some hair." Who says you can't die from embarrassment?

Whether it was the children's imagination or not — the dust was still coming in stifling puffs, making sense of their complaints. I wondered how much dirt we would consume before becoming as hardened as adobe bricks.

"We might as well go to bed. We will be better off than sitting here breathing dust all night," my weary husband announced.

We helped the children remove their clothing to get ready for bed, tucked them under the covers and formed a tent over their heads with a sheet to keep the dust from suffocating them.

"My head is killing me," I told Bob later. "I can't sleep."

He left our bed. I heard him rummaging through the dresser drawer. He returned with one of his Sunday linen handkerchiefs dripping water and spread it over my face.

The next morning, we awoke to a strange brown world . The beds, floor, furniture, curtains, walls, everything was covered with fine dust. The clothing we had exchanged for sleeping garments lay in forlorn-looking stacks, dusty heaps unfit for another day's wear.

In the morning, the lingering smell of dust greeted us, but the sun was shining with the gleam of a new copper-bottom wash boiler. The cloudless blue sky gave no hint of anything out of the ordinary. A magic broom had swept the earth clean and free of debris and clutter. The chickens were singing. The cows mooed. Calves ma-a-ed. Horses neighed. The buildings stood in drifts of dust. Otherwise, everything appeared so normal. For a moment, I thought it must have been a hideous nightmare.

Moving cautiously across the floor to avoid stirring up the dust, I tip-toed to the kitchen. Every step made a crunchy squeak and left footprints. The kitchen resembled the aftermath of a volcanic eruption.

With a dry dishcloth, I brushed a cupful of dust as fine as cocoa from the top of the table where our meals were served. The brown coated cabinet, stove, and the gritty floor overwhelmed me. Pots and pans — everything had to be cleaned before I could even think of preparing breakfast.

I could not believe what my eyes beheld. The flour bin in the cabinet required one inch of brown soil to be scooped away before I could find white flour to make biscuits. I dumped the contents of the open sugar bowl, salt crock and all uncovered food in the pig-feeding bucket. Only jars, bottles, lidded containers were free of dust. Having to discard all of that food hurt because it would be a tremendous loss if winter came and there would be no money to replace it.

"Let's get the kids off to school and I'll help you clean up this mess," Bob told me after a hectic breakfast with coughs, sneezes and smarting eyes.

I fastened a small towel around my hair bun, a red bandana over my nose and mouth and tied a big faded apron around my waist. I was ready to commit mayhem on the job before us.

We shook clothing, bedding and curtains, hung them on the clothesline to air and freshen in the early morning. We made a quick decision to strip the house to the bare walls and put everything in the yard while we cleaned the empty rooms. It saved time and tempers.

"Oh, what I'd give for a vacuum cleaner and sweeper," I lamented.

"Wouldn't be much help without electricity, would it?" Bob had a broad grin on his severely dirt-streaked face, his nose clogged with dust.

"Smarty pants." I picked up a sofa pillow that had fallen to the floor behind the sofa and never missed until that moment and tossed it at him.

"Better luck next time," he retorted, threw me a kiss and went outside.

By evening everything was back in place. The windows gleamed in the western sunlight; the rooms were spotless, dustless and sweet smelling like a freshly-made strawbed. We had filled a large coal scuttle to the brim with reddish-brown powdered top soil.

We had three days to rest and enjoy our immaculate home with no hot wind and blowing dust. The wind switched from north to south and returned with furious vengeance to rival the first duststorm. Day after day the wind blew. We reached the point where we began to wonder how much more of this relentless punishment we could take and survive. . . trapped in the vast American Dust Bowl that covered over 50 million acres.

Shrivelling, blistering, dust-laden wind blew every day, sapping the last bit of moisture from the ground.

"The water situation looks desperate," Bob announced after

one of his frequent trips to the windmill. "The well pumps only dribbles of water into the stock tank. We're going to be forced to find some way to conserve every drop."

I had been mulling something over in my mind. Now was the time to present another one of my goofy ideas.

"Let's dig a cistern. When it rains, the large expanse of our new roof will collect gallons of water. We can also fill it with nice clean snow before melting time comes in the spring. In the early days in Oklahoma, my parents had a cistern complete with a charcoal filter and a pump on the back porch. The natural water was "gyppie," tasted terrible because of the high content of gypsum mineral. Add soap and it became as thick as buttermilk — like a product unfit for anything but laundry. After adding lye to break it, it was a life-saver for my mother."

"H-m-m-m-m. Hadn't thought of that," Bob said. "It would save time spent hauling water from our neighbor's spring. I'll dig. You work the bucket detail. Bring the clods to the top when the digging gets rough."

Well, I asked for it. We selected the appropriate place, not far from the back porch. The digging began.

I don't know why I thought about it, but that well-digging reminded me of a Civil War story my grandfather told me when I was a little girl.

Grandfather

A ruddy glow spread across grandpa's face like the first peep of the morning sun. He looked long and thoughtfully at his birthday cake with 80 tiny candles.

Margaret, the first daughter born to Anne's family, had baked the large rectangular layers in the same pans mother used to make biscuits each morning for our family of eight children.

With a quick catch of breath, grandpa finally spoke: "I'm a Yankee Doodle Dandy guy." A big smile washed across his face. He gave a sniff, grimaced a bit as he stood tall, squared his shoulders, thrust out his chest and saluted. He remembered how he did it years ago in the Army.

He was proud of his Fourth of July birthday; loved it as much as the red, white and blue of Independence Day. "The parades, the boom of the big bands, the clash of cymbals, the spine-tingling tweedle-dee of the fifes, the staccato rat-a-tat-tat of the snare drums was the best of the whole shebang," he declared.

I've seen him wipe a tear from his cheek with the back of his hand when the prancing snare drummers passed in the parade.

Grandpa, William Henry Dye, my maternal grandfather, was born July 4, 1841. He married Sarah Margaret Mitchell. His family consisted of two daughters — Evalena, eight years older than her sister, Anna Elizabeth, my mother. Twin boys were still-born, which left no male to perpetuate grandpa's family name.

"Once there might have been an O before my last name, but it probably was dumped in the Atlantic when my ancestors came over from Ireland," grandpa told me.

A little boy playing with the lambs in the bluegrass pastures of Kentucky, he never dreamed some day he would serve in a Civil War caused by a conflict in the United States of his beloved America.

He was neither a Yankee, nor was he the ostentatious Colonel type as depicted in "Gone with the Wind," and other stories of magnolia blossoms and honey suckle-twined fences dripping fragrance. He did not wear cream-colored trousers, a dark jacket splendored with brass buttons or carry an impressive cane with a gold lion's head. He detested goatees. "Why in thunderation would any man want to look like a billy goat?" expressed his unabashed opinion. I've seen him turn up his nose at the mention of mint julep.

"He's a true son of the 'ole Kentucky' tradition. God-fearing, honest as the day is long. First at work, last to quit with an endless flow of Irish wit and humor," his friends and neighbors agreed.

One of my best memories of him was near his 70th year. My mother insisted he was too old to stay alone while Addie, my step grandmother, spent each summer in Chicago with her three motherless grandchildren from a former marriage.

After much discussion, I was given the honor of being grandpa's companion and care giver in gandma's absence. I was a gangling, stringy-haired, freckled-face 12-year-old tom-boyish girl.

That first morning after grandma left, grandpa built a fire in the square, squatty stove with a side door oven. I was supposed to make breakfast while he milked Flossy, tossed corn to the pig and fed the prize speckled chickens. I was anxious to try hard to please my grandpa.

I spied grandma's black and white checked-gingham apron, the one with the turkey-red cross stitching above the hem, hanging behind the kitchen door. I tied it around my questionable middle and began to hustle around as I had seen her do many times.

First, I poured water in the blue and white granite coffee pot, tossed a hand full of coffee in it as I had seen grandmother do, and tried to think what came next to prepare breakfast for the first time in my life..

I grabbed a heavy iron skille, set it down hard on a *c-o-l-d* stove. I had forgotten the fire needed attention as we had natural gas in our home since I was seven years old.

Peeking into the firebox, I saw the smoking wood and lumps of coal, but no fire. Reaching for a can of kerosene on the floor, I pulled the gumdrop cork from the spout and dashed a few big drops on the wood and coal. I took a match from a little black box on the nearby wall, struck it on the stove lid, and tossed it in the firebox. A hissing sound, like the warning of a rattlesnake, came first, followed by a big bang that rattled the stove caps. With a loud whoosh, flames shot toward the ceiling. It scared the pee out of me. Fortunately, I had gumption enough to slam the lid over the gaping hole spewing hot flames. The overhead flash disappeared and the fire began to crackle and burn just before I blacked out for a short period.

What if I had caught grandma's apron or my dress on fire? What if I had burned the house down? What if? What ifs filled every thought.

Shaking until my knees knocked, I leaned against the old kitchen cabinet with the underneath bins of flour and sugar. Over the countertop, a shelf with a cover of white butcher paper cut with grandma's pinking scissors to form pretty scallops complimented an array of her spices and home-made vinegars — basil, tarragon, rosemary and bottles of tiny red peppers. The countertop displayed a jug of sorghum molasses, a bucket of lard, a canister of coffee, another one for brown sugar, soda, baking powder and a small blue crock with salt for pinches to season her cooking. A recipe for pickled peaches with a warning to be sure to use Chinese Cling peaches was pinned to one scallop.

As soon as I could control my wobbly legs, I fetched a slab of home-cured bacon from the small ice box. The first slice cut was as thin as the tissue I used to make paper doll dresses. The next slice had two ends with enough middle to hold it together. For a second or two, I considered throwing the slices in the fire and starting over again, but decided it was almost time for grandpa to be coming to the house. The next try, somewhat better, had a slice with a lump of fat on one end. I finally managed to cut enough bacon to cover the bottom of the skillet.

With the table set and breakfast almost ready, I loved the grown-up feeling of accomplishment and pride I was experiencing. It's almost like I am a real lady doing things in my very own kitchen, I thought.

Grandpa came into the kitchen while I was scrambling eggs in too much bacon drippings. The room was cozy with the aroma of coffee, bacon and warmed-over biscuits I found in the pie cupboard where grandma had left them.

"Sure smells good," grandpa said. He glanced at my barefeet peeking from underneath grandma's long apron and smiled. He poured water from the dipper into a gray-granite washpan, doused his face with the water cupped in his hands and dried them on the roller towel hanging by the dining room door.

Later at the table, he took a bite of food, stopped chewing for a second, and squinted one eye.

"Huh! I get a faint taste of kerosene."

Did I splash a drop or two of kerosene in the skillet? The thought brought me to near panic. Perhaps he could guess what I had done with the kerosene can.

Pretending I didn't hear him, I became deeply absorbed in slathering Damson plum jam on my buttered biscuit.

"Sure is a good breakfast," he said as he folded his napkin, pulled it through the silver ring by his plate. Then he placed his big warm hand over mine on the table and smiled a sweet smile...

I thought he was old at that time. His shoulders sagged a bit from the weight of his years. But he held his head high and walked proudly in spite of "this confounded rheumatism in my back." His mustache was small and neatly trimmed. The shape of his beard, the same gun-metal gray of his hair, reminded me of the slobber bib mothers tied under their baby's chin during teething time.

A Baptist deacon, the Sunday morning greeter of the young and the old, he passed out hymn books at the small church door. He was admired and respected by the town folk. Out of his deep concern for humanity, he was extremely generous and quick "to pass the hat" for every worthy cause. Like the time the youngest of Mrs. Barker's five children was playing with a box of matches and started a fire. With their home completely destroyed, they were left homeless and penniless. Another time, grandma Lucas' horse ran away when it became frightened by a loud blast from a local train whistle. She escaped with minor injuries but the one-horse buggy overturned and splintered like kindling. The hat was passed and grandma was overwhelmed with a new carriage.

Although grandpa lived in the midwest for many years, he still remembered "old Kentucky" traditions and her distilleries. As soon as the nippy weather of fall arrived, he ordered four quarts of his favorite ingredient for his morning toddy — a concoction of rock candy, FOUR ROSES and a "wee bit of hot water."

"It's har-r-r-d to take, but it's good for my cough," I heard him tell my Uncle Bill. He gave him a wink, a little sniff, a toss of his elbow to assimilate a nudge; it was a trick I had seen him do many times to suggest a shared secret or big joke.

I could not recall any coughing spells, maybe a little hack-hack once in awhile. That nudge and wink bothered me — a lot. I had to know. One day, I approached him fearlessly and trustingly.

"Grandpa, did you ever get drunk?"

"Yes. Once when I was a young sprout," he answered without hesitation.

"Did you know what you were doing when you were drunk?"

"Yes. That's one of the worst things about drunkenness. You know what you're doing. You just don't give a darn."

That satisfied me. It made me feel as happy as the time I gave mother my brand new muslin drawers with the tiny blue bows on the leg band for a little girl's burial clothes. I could not endure the thought that my grandpa, who I loved so dearly, would ever do anything dishonorable or mean.

His stories always fascinated me and held me in a spell of wonderment. He showed me a tin-type picture of a beautiful young woman. Her dark hair carefully parted in the middle and pulled back softly where tiny curling scolders touched her ears and neck. Jeweled earrings dangled over her Venetian lace collar. She held a single white rose in her hand.

I looked at the picture a long time as he watched the expression on my face.

After awhile, he spoke: "She was my Civil War sweetheart - your grandmother, who passed away when your mother was a little girl."

"I betcha' you took this picture to the war with you."

"Sure did, Thelma. Right here. He placed his hand over his heart and patted it.

He enlisted as a drummer boy when he was 17 and was called for duty at 18. He was a robust young fellow who was huskier than most of his peers. One time, after a fierce battle, officers who had observed grandpa's demeanor and raw courage recruited him to serve with a small contingent of "bushwackers." The Army's supply of wagons, mules, horses and equipment was badly depleted. There was a drastic need for replacements. The "whackers" were ordered to scout for contraband and supplies anywhere they could be found, confiscated and brought back to the regiment base for immediate use.

Hidden by trees, bushes and underbrush, the recruits moved cautiously through the wooded area.

Alerted by the crackle of dry twigs under their feet, the shrill scolding of a bluejay, the sudden chatter of squirrels in trees overhead brought them to a sudden halt.

"What's that?"

The recruits froze in their position and listened. Someone whispered in an almost inaudible tone.

"Sounds like a scream — probably a mountain lion or a wildcat in a nearby den."

"Naw, it's different. There ain't no mountain lions here."

They heard it again. This time it came clear, a piercing scream followed by muffled sobs. They waited.

Peering through the underbrush of thick oak trees, they spotted two black mules grazing in an enclosed pasture. A split-rail fence zig-zagged like a sidewinder rattlesnake to form the boundary line of the property. The mules were immediately suspected as being hidden contraband. They had probably been spooked by the earth-shaking boom of the cannons or fire of the guns, causing them to bolt and run away. Or, it could be a simple matter of legal ownership.

"War is war. Orders are orders. Contraband or confiscation, either way. We're taking the mules," the officer in charge announced.

They followed the screams and stumbled upon a crude log cabin partly hidden by tall trees. White smoke from a jagged-rock chimney cut into the blue autumn sky. It was dangerously close to their surveillance position. The men separated. One half remained in position to secure the vantage point; the others searched for signs of possible entrapment.

They spied the woman first. Her blue calico dress "appeared

to have spent too many days in the sun and too few on the washboard," grandpa told me. "When possum hunting was more important than hauling wash water from the crick, that accounted for a lot of dirty duds," he added with a smile.

She drew the ragged sleeve of her dress across her face, gave an overturned bucket a kick, which sent it rattling toward a pile of fresh earth. Apparently, a well was being dug as mounds of soil, shovels, buckets, an axe, ropes, tools and a brown jug with a corncob stopper were scattered around the yard.

At the rattle of the bucket, a burly mountain man bounded through the open door of the cabin.

"Get that bucket and go back to work 'er I'll give you something to bawl about," he shouted.

"I tell you, that scoundrel couldn't have looked worse had he been in a tussle with a she-bear. His buckskin britches looked like he'd whacked them off with sheep shears after he'd waded a muddy crick in time of high water." Grandpa was really wound up with his story.

"Sassin' me again, huh?" The man hit the woman with a blow that sent her reeling out of his reach.

"You bastard!" grandpa yelled. "What in thunderation do you think you're doing?" Grandpa became so enraged, he failed to wait for an all-clear signal from the guards and was later reprimanded.

"Any man with two feet of guts would not tolerate a thing like that. I learned early in life real men respected their women, held them in high esteem.

"Well," he continued. "I grabbed that son-of-gun by the collar, swung him around and gave him an upper cut to the jaw."

Shocked by the blow and the unexpected intrusion of his property, the mountain man staggered backward. He recovered quickly. Fists flew as they exchanged hard licks. Raspy breathing and grunts followed the thud of the heavy body blows. Shouts of encouragement came from grandpa's comrades and were echoed back from the surrounding hills.

"That scoundrel was no fair match," grandpa said. "Days of clearing timber, log rolling, fence and cabin building had seasoned him. And another thing, Thelma. You can't reason with your fists. There's no honor in fighting a drunk. I knew he could make mincemeat of me if he got that ax by the dirt pile. So, I hauled off, gave him a shove that sent him heels over head into the well, where he could finish his digging."

Grandpa inspected his skinned and bleeding knuckles; tweaked his nose to determine if it was broken. That done, he brushed the dirt from his trousers and rearranged his jacket.

"In one unguarded moment, that frail-looking little woman, who stood there watching our squabble, picked up a shovel from the ground and knocked me flatter than a piece of Army-rationed hardtack."

It took about two minutes for grandpa, shocked and dazed, to scramble to his feet and assume a steady stance. Once again, he brushed and rearranged his clothing and joined the other bushwhackers.

As they led the confiscated mules back to their headquarters, he appraised his combat with a chuckle:

"I learned a good lesson, fellows. If ever again I'm caught in a husband-and-wife spat, I'll say: 'Go to it, cat and dog. You're no kin.' and I'll start making tracks in the opposite direction."

Night after night, grandpa and I read together. He sat in his easy chair, an old swing rocker covered in fading tapestry. The headrest displayed one of Addie's crocheted antimacassar to keep the chair tidy. I sat opposite him on the red mohair sofa with arms that could be lowered for napping. Between us, the fruit-wood table boasted brass claws grasping large glass balls. Sometimes, the wick on the table lamp burned to a char. The smoke, laced with the odor of kerosene, shed its overworked vengeance over the room. Grandpa's briarwood pipe rested on the table as it turned cold and was forgotten.

Once he looked up from the book he was reading. His glasses rested on the tip of his nose. He peered over them with sleepy eyes. I thought he was going to read a few lines from his book by one of his old friends, "Charlie Dickens or Bill Shakespeare." He spoke of them with such reverence, I wondered if they were some of our dead kinfolk.

"Listen, Thelma. Here's what old Bill Shakespeare said: 'All the world is a stage. We are merely the players.'"

He stirred my curiosity and interest when he introduced me to the books and characters he loved. If he saw a questioning look on my face, he stopped to explain the passage. I learned to enjoy ordinary people doing extraordinary things in simple or sometimes in somewhat questionable ways. His interest, patience and endurance helped to remove the bulwark between my youth and the big world beyond my comprehension.

"Listen and read with your heart," he told me. "It makes understanding better. The way we handle emotions in our life helps to make us who we are," he volunteered.

My parents could not have given me the quality time and undivided attention he gave to me. With a family of eight fast-developing children in a rapidly-changing world, precious time had to be shared.

In putting my book aside one night at bedtime, I felt a sharp pain, something I had never experienced previously as I placed my hand on my chest. To my amazement, I found two small lumps growing there. I couldn't tell anyone, much less grandpa. Although he had always been there for me, encouraging me in all of my endeavors, comforting me in my failures, urging me to smile and try again, this was a private matter.

From that day I knew never again would I have the insatiable desire for more paper dolls cut from mother's McCalls magazine or for more and more Elsie Dinsmore books. My time spent with my grandfather left beautiful memories to recall and cherish always.

Closure

From dust-veiled dawn to night fall, when the chill deep in the earth seeps upward through the cracks in the dry ground, we fought dust and despair.

Black Sunday was the day the skin of the earth began to peel. The top soil from Illinois, Iowa, Nebraska blew from the rich corn belt of America. Wheat-field land, stripped from Kansas fields, blended with the smokey rust color of Oklahoma's red clay farms. Added to the mix: alkali dust from mine-tailings in Utah and Arizona seemed to form a conspiracy to bury us. Neighboring Baca County's over-plowed fields were burying themselves without any help. There seemed to be no end to the falling mantle.

Despair lurked around every corner, threatening to demoralize us, to destroy our hopes and dreams for the future.

"It's time to check the well," Bob told me one day when hot wind calmed briefly.

"What is that eerie sound coming from the windmill," I asked as we inspected green slimy traces of water in an empty stock tank.

"That, my dear, is the cry of a drying well. The water table has dropped. There's no water to keep the sucker-rod leathers wet — suction is needed to draw the water upward through the metal pipes, causing the alternate sounds of screeching and moaning. I'm going to tether the fan to protect the gears. The well is dead."

I didn't understand much of the mechanics of a functioning or nonfunctioning well, but I did understand a *dying well*. I shuddered as I thought of the loss and impending doom.

The overturned water barrel, the lead pipe to the tank, lay on the ground. The farm gate was a tangled mess of barbed wire and wooden staves; the flattened fence showed scrounging and desperation of frantic animals.

"That's the second time this week the range horses have clobbered our place," my husband commented as he pounded staples into fence posts.

In the early days, if a farmer owned a seriously-injured horse, or one considered unfit for the rugged work of the farm, he was termed too old for work and of no value.

Often, these almost-human animals with names like Major, Freckles, Lady Rainbow, Pancho and Prince, were beloved pets which brought families from Missouri and faraway places.

Giving them their freedom was an act of love and appreciation— freedom from galling collars, chaffing binding harnesses and aching muscles. Freedom to roam the verdant pastures of belly-high buffalo grass, to drink from shallows, ditches and small creeks formed from melting snow and early rains.

Those were "the good ole' days" of hard work, good times with friends and neighbors and long friendships that would last forever. But time passed and the calendar recorded the days — dust storm — hot winds — drying wells — cow died, dust ball in stomach — Mr. White's boy with dust pneumonia — all combined to promote a hellish period of unrivaled destruction.

"Mother! A dust is coming down the road."

I wished I had a load of hay for every time they called that warning.

Many times, I had a clothesline full of fresh-laundered white and colored clothing billowing in the breeze — the first clear day in weeks.

Windows and doors were opened wide to welcome clean fresh air. The backyard fence held an array of forlorn-looking over beaten rugs to be refreshed by the sunshine.

The children played in the yard, the first barefoot day they could enjoy without blistered feet from the hard hot ground.

One thing I did not need at this moment was another duster as I began to snatch the clothes from the line. I thought of Claudia Bean, one of the last neighbors left in an area of abandoned homes. Maybe she was coming to visit for cheer, a good visit with laughs and remembrances. Her husband was gone — went to California to find work. Bob and I often wondered if these daddies and husbands would ever reunite with their families in a world filled with uncertainty, perilous times, temptations and hopelessness. So many women left behind with families needing encouragement, times spent in less stressful situations.

The moving cloud of dust could be a neighbor who needed help or another whirlwind gathering dust in its waning gyrations. It could be another group of range horses growing in numbers daily. This time, it was not a matter of a faithful worker being retired to enjoy the simple life, work-free, all needs supplied for the remainder of life.

This time, they were forced to go. They were useless because the fields were gone; blown away by the hots winds. Worthless because they had lost all value on the farms and in a gutted market. Unwanted because there was no feed, no water, no hope, at present, for a future where they would be reunited with their owners.

As the dust cloud approached, we could distinguish a blended mass of motley colors — dirty, shaggy, and knotted — dead horses walking, walking and walking, too emaciated, too weak, without incentive to search for feed and water anymore. They plodded back and forth, up and down the country lanes in numb continuity, breathing a lung-clogged death of their own making.

"Now that the well is gone, we should try to sell our cattle and horses before prices drop again," Bob told me in a voice that sounded like someone who is announcing plans for the last rites of a family member. "They're still in pretty good shape."

I hated to part with the livestock, although Bob assured me we would replace them "when things get better." I can't say, truthfully, I learned to love those mules, Jack and Joe, but I can say now that they were leaving for an unknown future, the skittish feeling I experienced when they opened their mouths with one of their blatant he-haws had changed. I appreciated their loyalty, their hard work, with steadfast dependable patience as they responded to their master's commands in language learned from people association. I would miss Maude and her baby mule-colt, also the first-born of our horse family.

Humdrum days passed like melting icicles that once hung from the roof. There seemed to be no excitement or enthusiasm for school. No rush to be first to give a play-by-play account of the day's activity. Mr. Holderman, the new teacher, who boarded with us, appeared to be as lethargic as some of his students.

Clang, clang, the four o'clock school bell announced the end of another day. Mr. Holderman brought the children home from school Monday through Friday, when he made a fast disappearance, antsy to leave a dusty school room and the few students who were becoming restless, coughing and sneezing with watery eyes and runny noses, who showed very little enthusiasm for books or outside play.

Jean came home one afternoon complaining of a severe headache. By the next morning, two lumps the size of nut halves appeared on her forehead over her eyes.

"We can't fool around with something like this — home remedies are out," Bob announced. "We'll take her to a doctor in Trinidad."

After making arrangements with a neighbor and single mother, Inez Rhodes, and her daughter, Betty, stayed with Bobby and June. Donny, Jean and I made the trip. Had it not been for Jean's illness, it would be blessed relief to go to the mountains where the air was clean, streets dust-free, white houses among the green trees beside the trickle of the Purgatory River in summertime.

After examining Jean, the doctor became very serious.

"Mr. Doak, your daughter's problem is related to the dust storms in the East End. Unless you get your family out of there, you could lose them. Every day we see more and more symptoms of dust pneumonia and the beginning of an epidemic that could equal the 1918 flu in that dust-bowl area. Vets have found dustballs in cattle, lung trouble in horses."

We returned home tired, weary, numb. What next? What, where, how could all of this be happening to us."

"A very important-looking man came to see you, Mr. Doak. He was dressed in a black suit, white shirt and shiny shoes," Inez reported to my husband upon our return home. "He said he'd come back next week."

We did not spend much time thinking about the man with the shiny black shoes. We were trying to make some sense of what the future held for us, and how to make a start towards its fruition.

"Hello, Lon," Bob said a week later. "What are you up to these days?" He was an old friends of the early homestead days, minus the usual chit-chat of farm life, community gossip and news of mutual friends. He appeared cool, very much a businessman on an important mission — not the Lon Robertson he knew from the old days.

"Bob, I'm a representative of the government." He showed his credentials. "I understand you have a federal loan on your land." He said this as though he didn't know who had federal loans, which included almost all of the East End farmers. "After much study and research, the government is going to use its power of eminent domain to foreclose all loans and reclaim the land."

Just like that — everything was gone. The land, the house my father and brother built, our livestock, the dead well built by the

$1,000 loan at 4 percent for 30 years. And the promise Uncle Sam made to the soldiers who marched away during World War I. "We will forego any time limit owed. A deed will be granted for complete ownership of your homestead after service rendered."

We owed a debt. We paid it: Paid it with everything we had.

As an absentee owner, the share croppers paid the interest on the loan each year. We had 30 years to repay the loan made when Bob homesteaded in the early 1900s, a young man who came from college to hard times and a jobless period. He and young friends decided homesteading would be interesting fun and give them a start in life.

It was time to go — moving day again. There was little to move for this trip; a truckload of furniture that showed five years of memories, dreams delayed, hope for the good life suspended forever.

I even wished for the battered green and yellow truck that brought us from Texas to the farm. Curtis, an old friend of early days, who hauled freight for the stores in Kim, volunteered to move us since he was traveling empty to Trinidad.

Our four children were huddled in the back seat of the car, quiet, not knowing what to expect next since the county clerk had asked Bob to come for an interview. There had been so little time to explain fully to the children what was happening. Not wanting to upset them, we failed to prepare them for another change, which was a mistake.

"Would you like to take one more look at our home?" Bob asked as he stopped the car at the big gate.

Through a haze of tears I tried to hide, I did not see the unfinished home we were leaving forever. I saw as if it were a dream nestled in my heart. I could see the beautiful pink, tan and brown blended rock-covered house gleaming in a green pasture, lush, juicy, dotted with red and white Hereford cattle. A new windmill pumped a steady flow of clear cool water. Trees and flowers, whose fragrance was making me dizzy, grew in the yard. There were our children, grown, smiling and happy as they entertained friends from college on a summer vacation.

Not one word could I utter. My eyes were riveted on the picture I was seeing in my mind, and, for fear of an emotional collapse overtaking me, I looked at my husband, who had been with me all the way. The children were quiet, with no apparent show of understanding.

Uncle Sam giveth. By eminent domain, Uncle Sam taketh away. This is the last journey to the mountains from our home. The "East End" is gone.

Bob took his hand from the steering wheel, placed it on my knee. His hazel eyes met mine: "Bet you can't spell Winnipesaukee."